PAINTING IN WATERCOLOUR

PRACTICAL TECHNIQUES AND PROJECTS FOR BEGINNERS

PAINTING IN WATERCOLOUR

PRACTICAL TECHNIQUES AND PROJECTS FOR BEGINNERS

All the basics shown step by step: mixing, brush strokes, masking out, glazing, wet into wet, drybrush painting, washes, resists, stippling, sponging, light to dark, sgraffito and more

WENDY JELBERT AND IAN SIDAWAY

southwater

This edition is published by Southwater,
an imprint of Anness Publishing Ltd, Blaby Road, Wigston,
Leicestershire LE18 4SE; info@anness.com

www.southwaterbooks.com; www.annesspublishing.com

If you like the images in this book and would like
to investigate using them for publishing, promotions
or advertising, please visit our website
www.practicalpictures.com for more information.

Publisher: Joanna Lorenz
Editorial Director: Helen Sudell
Senior Editor: Sarah Ainley
Editor: Elizabeth Woodland
Consultant Editor: Sarah Hoggett
Photographers: George Taylor and Nigel Cheffers-Heard
Designer: Nigel Partridge
Illustrator: Ian Sidaway
Project contributors: Ray Balkwill, Diana Constance,
Joe Francis Dowden, Paul Dyson, Abigail Edgar,
Wendy Jelbert, Melvyn Petterson, Paul Robinson,
Ian Sidaway, Albany Wiseman
Production Controller: Darren Price

© Anness Publishing Ltd 2012

A CIP catalogue record for this book is available
from the British Library.

Previously published as *Watercolour Painting*

PUBLISHER'S NOTE

Although the advice and information in this book are
believed to be accurate and true at the time of going
to press, neither the authors nor the publisher can accept any
legal responsibility or liability for any errors or omissions that
may have been made nor for any inaccuracies nor for any
loss, harm or injury that comes about from following
instructions or advice in this book.

ACKNOWLEDGEMENTS

The publishers and authors are grateful to **Daler-Rowney UK**
and **Turnham Arts and Crafts** for their generous loan of
materials for the photography.

In addition, special thanks must go to the following
watercolour artists for their step-by-step demonstrations:
t = top, b = bottom, l = left, r = right, c = centre.
Diana Constance: pages 40–41; **Paul Dyson:** pages 45,
Melvyn Petterson: pages 58–59; 61–63; 64–67; 68–71;
75(b)–77; 80–83; **Ian Sidaway:** pages 24–25; 28; 32–3; 44;
46–47; 50–51; 52 (tl, tr, cl, cr); 54 (tl, tr); 56 (tl, tr); 60;
72–73; 74–5 (t); 78–79; **Albany Wiseman:** pages 26–27; 29;
42–43; 52–53; 54–55; 56–57.

Copyright paintings and photographs are reproduced in this
book by kind permission of the following:
t = top, b = bottom, l = left, r = right, c = centre.
Paul Dyson: pages 20, 90, 91 (t); **Trudy Friend:** pages 21 (t);
Sarah Hoggett: pages 58 (bl); 61 (tl); 64 (b);
Wendy Jelbert: pages 21 (b); 91 (br); **Ian Sidaway:** pages
91 (bl); 92–93; 94–95(t); **George Taylor:** 28 (b).

Contents

Introduction

Watercolour painting is a creative, absorbing and enjoyable craft. It takes time and practice, but you will be rewarded with wonderful and satisfying results. As well as explaining all the techniques involved in watercolour painting, this book contains 25 step-by-step practice exercises designed to build confidence and to allow the skills to be put into practice as they are learned. A delightful practice manual for all beginners who enjoy painting with watercolour.

Paints

Watercolour paints are available in two main forms: pans, which are compressed blocks of colour that need to be brushed with water in order to release the colour, and tubes of moist paint. The same finely powdered pigments bound with gum-arabic solution are used to make both types. The pigments provide the colour, while the gum arabic allows the paint to adhere to the paper surface, even when highly diluted with water.

Both pans and tubes can be bought in sets or singly. Pans are available as full pans and half pans, the only difference is size. If there are certain colours that you use only infrequently, buy half pans. Tubes range in size from 5–20ml (0.17–0.66 fl oz).

It is a matter of personal preference whether you use pans or tubes. The advantage of pans is that they can be slotted into a paintbox, making them easily portable, and this is something to consider if you often paint on location. Tubes, on the other hand, are often better if you need to make a large amount of colour for a wash, although it is easy to squeeze out more paint than you need, which is wasteful. You also need to remember to replace the caps of tube colours immediately, otherwise the paint will harden and become unusable.

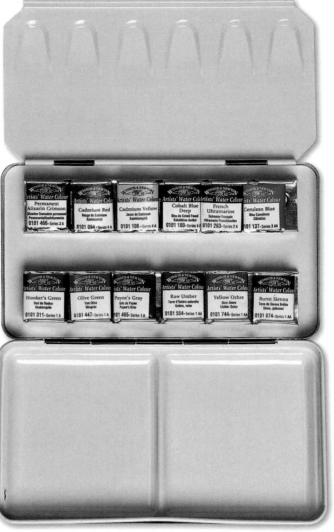

◄ Paintbox
You can buy paintboxes that are already filled with a selection of colours, or empty boxes that you then fill with colours of your own choice. The model shown here is for pans of paint, but you can also buy ones with spaces for tube colours.

Tubes ▲
Tubes of watercolour paint are available in different sizes. It is worth buying the larger sizes for colours that you think you will use frequently.

Gouache paint ▲
This is a kind of water-based paint. Unlike pure watercolour, it is opaque, although the techniques and equipment used for gouache are similar to those used for watercolour. White gouache, in particular, is often used in conjunction with pure watercolour, both to add small highlights and to mix with watercolour to make pale, opaque colours.

Palettes

Even if you usually mix colours in the lid of your paintbox, it is useful to have one or two separate palettes as well, particularly when you want to mix a large quantity of a wash. There are several shapes and sizes available, but two of the most common are the segmented round palette and the slanted-well tile.

Palettes are made from white ceramic or plastic. Although plastic is lightweight, which is an advantage when you need to carry your materials for painting on location, it is also slightly porous and will become stained over time.

For an inexpensive alternative, look out for white china saucers and plates in charity shops or jumble (rummage) sales. They must be white, as you would be able to see any other colour through the transparent paint, which would make it difficult to judge the colour or tone being mixed. Old teacups and bowls are good if you need to mix large quantities.

Pigment does settle, so remember to stir the wash in your palette from time to time to ensure that it is evenly dispersed. Always wash your palette thoroughly after use to prevent dried paint residue from muddying subsequent mixes.

Field box ▲
Most of the major manufacturers sell field boxes specifically for use on location, which include a small brush and perhaps a sponge as well as a selection of paints.

◄ **Segmented round palette**
This kind of palette, which is sometimes referred to as a chrysanthemum palette because of its flower-like shape, has deep wells that are perfect for mixing large washes.

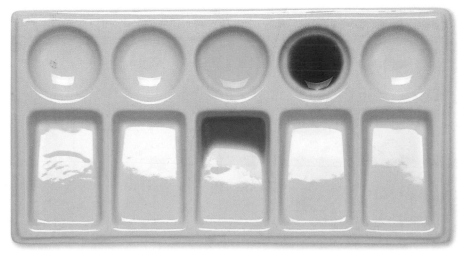

◄ **Slanted-well tile palette**
This type of palette is useful for mixing two or more colours together: place each colour in one of the round wells at one end of the palette and transfer a little on your brush to one of the flat, slightly sloping sections.

Grades of paint

There are two grades of watercolour paint: artists' and students' quality. Artists' quality paints are the more expensive, because they contain a high proportion of good-quality pigments. Students' quality paints contain less pure pigment and more fillers, and are usually available in a smaller range of colours than artists' quality paints.

If you come across the word "hue" in a paint name, it indicates that the paint contains cheaper alternatives to the real pigment. Generally speaking, you get what you pay for: artists' quality paints tend to produce more subtle mixtures of colours.

The other thing that you need to think about when buying paints is their permanence. The label or the manufacturer's catalogue should give you the permanency rating. In the United Kingdom, the permanency ratings are class AA (extremely permanent), class A (durable), class B (moderate) and class C (fugitive). The ASTM (American Society for Testing and Materials) codes for lightfastness are ASTM I (excellent), ASTM II (very good), and ASTM III (not sufficiently lightfast).

Some pigments, such as alizarin crimson and viridian, stain more than others: they penetrate the fibres of the paper and cannot be removed.

Finally, although we always think of watercolour as being transparent, you should be aware that some pigments are actually slightly opaque and will impart a degree of opacity to any colours with which they are mixed. These so-called opaque pigments include all the cadmium colours and cerulean blue.

Characteristics of paint ▼
Different pigments have different characteristics. The only way to learn about them is to use them and see how they behave, both singly and in combination with other colours. The chart below shows the characteristics of some of the most popular watercolour paints.

Transparent

Ultramarine blue Hooker's green Raw umber

Opaque

Cadmium red Cadmium yellow Yellow ochre

Staining

Alizarin crimson Viridian Gamboge

Judging colours

It is not always possible to judge the colour of paints simply by looking at the pans in your palette, as they often look dark. In fact, it is very easy to dip your brush into the wrong pan by mistake, so always check before you apply the brush to the paper.

Even when you have mixed a wash in your palette, appearances can be deceptive, as watercolour paint always looks lighter when it is dry. The only way to be sure what colour or tone you have mixed is to apply it to paper and let it dry. It is always best to build up tones gradually until you get the effect you want. The more you practise, the better you will get at anticipating results.

Appearances can be deceptive ▼
These two pans look very dark, almost black. In fact, one is Payne's grey and the other a bright ultramarine blue.

Test your colours ▼
Keep a piece of scrap paper next to you as you work so that you can test your colour mixes before you apply them to your painting.

What colours to choose?

With so many colours to choose from (some manufacturers offer as many as 100 artists' quality paints and up to 50 students' quality), how do you decide which ones to buy?

Although art supply stores and catalogues contain rainbow-like selections of every colour imaginable, the most important thing to realize is that you don't need to buy a huge range. You might choose to produce a painting entirely from ready-made colours, but learning how to mix your own will give you far more scope and is far more economical.

Some artists choose to work with a very limited palette of as few as five or six colours, creating astonishingly subtle variations in hue and tone in the process. Start with a few colours and learn as much as you can about them before you add to your range. In practice, most people find that a

range of 12–20 colours enables them to mix pretty much anything that they could wish for.

As you gain more experience, you will probably find that you discard certain colours in favour of others: this is all part of the learning process. Set aside some time to experiment and see how many colours and tones you can create by mixing two, or even three, colours together.

Above all, keep a note of any mixes that you particularly like, or find useful for certain subjects (such as trees, skies or water) so that you can recreate them in the future. Remember, however, that the more colours you combine, the more risk there is that the resultant mixes will look muddy and dull: one of the received wisdoms in pure watercolour painting is that you should not mix more than three colours together at any one time.

As always, your exact choice of colours is largely a matter of personal preference, but a good "starter palette" should contain at least one of each of the three primary colours (red, yellow and blue); in fact, it's helpful to have one blue with a warm bias, such as ultramarine blue, and one that is slightly cooler, such as cerulean. Earth pigments such as raw and burnt umber and raw and burnt sienna are useful for mixing neutral browns and greys. Although you can mix your own greens, versatile ready-mixed greens include viridian, Hooker's green and sap green. Payne's grey is a good colour to mix with other colours for cast shadows.

Suggested starter palette ▼
The palette shown below is a versatile selection of colours that will enable you to create a wide range of mixes.

Cerulean blue   Ultramarine blue   Cadmium red   Cadmium yellow

Raw umber   Burnt umber   Raw sienna   Burnt sienna

Payne's grey   Hooker's green   Alizarin crimson   Yellow ochre

Papers

There are three main types of watercolour paper: hot-pressed (HP), NOT, and rough. Hot-pressed paper is best for drawing and detailed work; it is very smooth to the touch. NOT surface, meaning not hot-pressed (cold-pressed), has a slight texture. Rough paper has a prominent "tooth"; when a wash is laid over it, some of the deep cavities are left unfilled, giving a sparkle to the painting. The best papers are handmade from pure linen rag and the quality is reflected in the price.

Good-quality paper has a right and a wrong side. The right side is coated with size, which is receptive to watercolour applications. To find out which side to use, hold the paper up to the light and look for the water mark on the right side.

Watercolour paper is available in rolls, sheets, and pads and blocks of various sizes. Pads are either spiral bound or glued; blocks are glued on all sides to keep the paper flat until you need to remove a sheet. Pads and blocks are more practical for location work and quick sketches.

Types of paper ▼
From left to right: hot-pressed (HP), NOT and rough watercolour papers. Hot-pressed paper has a very smooth surface, while the other two are progressively more textured.

Tinted papers ▼
Tinted papers are sometimes frowned upon by purists, but there are times when you want to establish an overall colour key; these ready-made tinted papers are a good alternative to laying an initial flat wash.

Duck-egg blue

Eggshell

Cream

Hot-pressed (HP)

NOT

Rough

Stretching paper

Papers come in different weights. The weight refers to the weight of a ream (500 sheets) and can vary from 90lb (185 grams per square metre or gsm) for lightweight papers to 300lb (640gsm) or more. The heavier the paper, the more readily it will take the water. Papers that are less than 140lb (300gsm) in weight need to be stretched before use, otherwise they will cockle when water is applied. First, the paper is soaked in water so that it expands; it is then taped or stapled to a board. As it dries it contracts, giving a taut surface that will not buckle when subsequent washes are applied.

1 Dip a sponge in clean water and wipe it over the paper, making sure you leave no part untouched.

2 Make sure a generous amount of water has been applied over the whole surface and that the paper is perfectly flat.

3 Moisten four lengths of gum strip and place one along each long side of the paper. (Only gummed brown-paper tape is suitable; masking tape will not adhere to damp paper.)

4 Repeat for the short edge of the paper. Leave to dry. (In order to be certain that the paper will not lift, some artists also staple it to the board.)

Brushes

A quick glance through any art supplier's catalogue will reveal a bewildering range of brushes, from outrageously expensive sable brushes to budget-range synthetics. Although you might be tempted to invest heavily and stock up on a vast selection, in all shapes and sizes, in practice you can get away with a small number: a large brush for laying a wash, a medium-sized brush for moderate washes and larger details, and a smaller brush for fine detail should be enough to begin with.

The two main shapes of brush are flat and round. Round brushes are perhaps the most useful general-purpose brushes. They hold a lot of paint, allowing you to lay down broad strokes of colour and washes, but they also come to a fine point for more precise marks. Flat brushes have a square, chisel-shaped end. These, too, can be used for broad washes, while the flat end is used for making clean-edged, linear marks.

Many artists use Chinese-style brushes similar to those used by calligraphers: like good-quality round brushes, they hold a lot of paint but also come to a fine point. You may also come across rigger brushes (round brushes with long hairs and a fine point), which are useful for fine lines and details, and spotter brushes (less common, with very short hairs), which tend to be used by miniaturists and other artists whose work involves painting fine, very precise details.

Brushes can be made from natural hair. Sable, which is obtained from the tail of the sable marten, a relative of the mink, is the best, and the best sables come from the Kolinsky region of northern Siberia. Camel, ox and squirrel hair are common, as are synthetic materials. Buy the best quality you can afford. Cheaper brushes may shed hairs or wear out more quickly, and they may not hold as much colour or come to a point. Look for seamless, corrosion-resistant ferrules: they hold the hairs tightly and will not tarnish. Also check whether they hold their shape well. Unfortunately, you can't always tell this when you buy brushes as they are often "dressed" with some kind of adhesive, which needs to be washed out before you use them, so that they hold their points.

Round brushes ▼

Most art stores stock round brushes ranging in size from the ultra-fine 000 right up to the rather fat size 12, although you will also find brushes that lie outside this range. To begin with, however, three brushes – one small, one medium and one large – will provide you with a versatile selection that should cover most eventualities. It is good practice to use the largest brush that you can for any given painting situation, so that you get into the habit of making broad, sweeping marks rather than tight, fussy ones.

Small round brush

Medium round brush

Large round brush

Large brushes ▼

Both flat brushes and mop brushes can be used to lay a wash over the paper ground. Flat brushes are wide and straight-edged, while mop brushes have large, round heads.

Flat brush

Mop brush

Other types of brush ▶

Your choice of brush is very much a matter of personal taste, so experiment to find out which ones you enjoy using. You will find that some suit your style of painting better than others. Shown here are some of the other types of brush that you might come across.

A rigger brush has long hairs and a very fine point, and is good for painting fine lines and details. A Chinese-style brush is good for flowing, calligraphic marks; it holds a lot of paint and keeps its shape well, making it a versatile brush. The flat edge of a chisel brush makes it a good choice for painting straight-edged shapes – when painting up to the edge of a building, for example. In a fan brush, the bristles are splayed out, and this makes it useful for drybrush work.

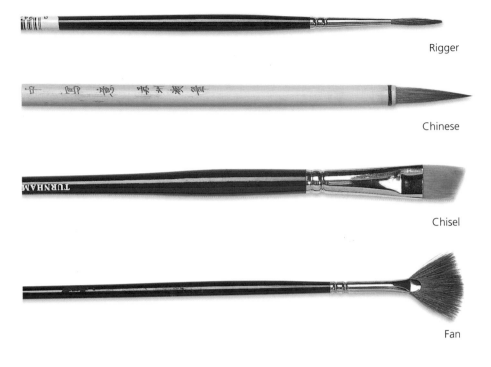

Rigger

Chinese

Chisel

Fan

Caring for brushes

Given the cost of good-quality brushes, it is worth taking the time and trouble to look after them properly in order to prolong their life.

You should always clean your brushes immediately after use. Gently rub a little liquid detergent into the hairs, working it in with your fingertips and working right up to the ferrule. Rinse in clean running water until all the paint has been removed.

Cleaning brushes ▼

No matter how carefully you rinse your brushes, liquid detergent is the only way to be sure that you have got rid of all paint residue.

Storing brushes ▶

After cleaning your brushes, squeeze the hairs to remove any excess water and then gently reshape the brush with your fingertips. Leave to dry. Store brushes upright in a jar to prevent the hairs from becoming bent as they dry.

> **Tips:** • When you are painting, try not to leave brushes standing in water as this can ruin both the hairs and the wooden handles.
> • When cleaning brushes, keep rinsing the brush under running water until the water runs clear. Make sure that any paint near the metal ferrule has been completely removed.
> • Do not be tempted to store newly cleaned and still-wet brushes in an airtight container as mildew can develop.
> • Moths are very keen on sable brushes, so if you need to store your brushes for any length of time, it is a good idea to use mothballs to act as a deterrent.

Pencils and pens

While there is no need to have more than a small selection, pencils and pens are valuable accessories in the artist's tool kit.

Pencils

The most common use of pencils in watercolour paintings is to make an initial underdrawing to map out the composition and put in the main lines of your subject as a guideline for when you come to apply the paint. It is very useful to keep a small selection of pencils to hand for this purpose.

Although graphite pencils range from 9B (very soft) to 9H (very hard), the more extreme choices are actually less useful: very soft pencils can smear while very hard ones make light, unimpressive marks. A more average HB and a 2B or 4B should be adequate for most underdrawings, depending on how strong you want the marks to be. It is also worth having a few very soft pencils in your collection to make quick tonal studies. Charcoal pencils and sticks are ideal.

Coloured pencils, too, are useful, and are particularly good for making colour notes when you are sketching on location. They are available in many colours but, unlike graphite pencils, only one degree of hardness.

You can also buy water-soluble pencils and crayons, both of which allow you to combine linear marks with the fluidity of watercolour washes. Easily portable, they are useful for location work. The range of colours is extensive, but many artists feel that they lack the subtlety of watercolour paints. Some brands seem to blend better than others, so experiment to find out which kinds you enjoy using.

Tip: If you wish to use water soluble pencils on location but do not want to carry the pencils, make heavy scribbles on paper in a range of colours: when you brush the scribbles with clean water you can pick up enough colour on the brush to use them as watercolour paints.

Pencils ▼

It is useful to keep a small range of pencils to hand for making tonal studies and underdrawings. For general usage, choose a medium hard pencil such as HB or 2B.

Charcoal pencil

HB graphite pencil

2B graphite pencil

Water-soluble pencils ▼

Water-soluble pencils can be used dry, to make clearly defined marks, or wet to create soft blends and colour mixes. To use a water-soluble pencil wet, either dip the tip in clean water or apply the pencil to the paper in the normal way and brush over the marks with a wet brush.

Blue

Red

Orange

Yellow

Green

Purple

◄ Crayons
These colour sticks are similar in consistency to hard pastels. Crayons are capable of much bolder effects than pencil, and are excellent for crisp, decisive lines and for areas of solid dark tone, as they can be sharpened to a point or broken into short lengths and used sideways. Bear in mind that crayons cannot be erased easily.

Pens

Pens are most frequently used in watercolour in the line-and-wash technique, in which linear detail is put in in ink on top of (or under) loose watercolour washes.

There are various kinds of pen suitable for this technique. Fountain pens have the advantage of having a reservoir to hold the ink (or are loaded with a cartridge of ink), which means that you don't have to keep stopping to reload, but many artists prefer the spontaneity and rougher lines of dip pens. Both have interchangeable nibs, allowing you to vary the width and character of the lines you make. You can also create different widths of line by turning the pen over and using the back of the nib. Technical drawing pens of the type used by architects and graphic designers deliver a line of uniform width. These are available in a range of sizes.

As far as inks are concerned, your choice is between waterproof and water-soluble. Once dry, waterproof ink marks will remain permanent even when watercolour paint is applied over the top. Water-soluble inks, on the other hand, will blur and spread.

Inks can be used at full strength or diluted with water to create different tones; you may want to use several dilutions of ink in the same painting. Black is the colour traditionally used in line and wash, but there are many other colours available; they do not, however, possess the lightfastness of watercolour pigments.

Waterproof black ink

Water-soluble sepia ink

Steel-nibbed dip pen

Technical drawing pen

Additional equipment

There are a few other pieces of equipment that you will probably find useful in your watercolour painting, ranging from things to secure your work to the drawing board and easels to support your painting to aids to specific painting techniques.

The most important thing is that the surface on which you are working must be completely flat and unable to wobble around as you work. If you use blocks of watercolour paper, then the block itself will provide enough support; you can simply rest it on a table or your knee. If you use sheets of watercolour paper, then they need to be firmly secured to a board. Buy firm boards that will not warp and buckle (45 x 60cm/18 x 24in is a useful size), and attach the paper to the board by means of gum strip or staples.

It is entirely a matter of personal preference as to whether or not you use an easel. There are several types on the market, but remember that watercolour paint is a very fluid liquid and can easily flow down the paper into areas that you don't want it to touch. Choose an easel that can be used flat and propped at only a slight angle. The upright easels used by oil painters are not really suitable for watercolour painting.

Other useful pieces of equipment include a scalpel or craft (utility) knife: the fine tip allows you to prise up pieces of masking tape that have become stuck down too firmly without damaging the paper. You can also use a scalpel to scratch off fine lines of paint – a technique known as sgraffito. Absorbent kitchen paper is invaluable for cleaning out paint palettes and lifting off or softening the colour before it dries.

As you develop your painting style and techniques, you may want to add other equipment to the basic items shown here. You will probably assemble a selection of props, from bowls, vases and other objects for still lifes, to pieces of fabric and papers to use as backgrounds. Similarly, you may want to set aside pictures or photographs that appeal to you for use as reference material. The only real limit to what you can use is your imagination.

Box easel ▼
This easel includes a handy side drawer in which you can store brushes and other paraphernalia, as well as adjustable bars so that it can hold various sizes of drawing board firmly in place. Some easels can only be set at very steep angles, which is unsuitable for watercolour, so do check before you buy.

Table easel ▼
This inexpensive table easel is more than adequate for most watercolourists' needs. Like the box easel it can be adjusted to a number of different angles, allowing you to alter the angle to suit the technique you are using. It can also be folded flat so that it can be stored neatly when it is not in use.

Gum strip ▲

Gummed brown-paper strip is essential for taping stretched lightweight watercolour paper to a board, to ensure that it does not buckle when the water is applied. Leave the paper stretched on the drawing board until you have finished your painting and the paint has dried, then simply cut it off, using a scalpel or craft (utility) knife and a metal ruler, and discard. Masking tape cannot be used in place of gum strip for the purpose of taping stretched watercolour paper.

Gum arabic ▲

Adding gum arabic to watercolour paint increases the viscosity of the paint and slows down the drying time. This gives you longer to work, which is often what you need when painting detail or referring to a reference photo while you are painting. Add a few drops of the gum arabic to your paint and stir to blend. Gum arabic also imparts a slight sheen on the paper, which can be useful for certain subjects, and it increases the intensity of the paint colour.

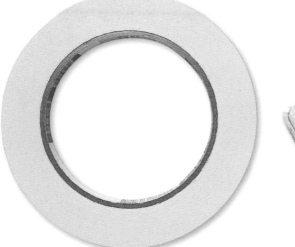

Masking fluid and masking tape ▲

Masking is one of the most basic techniques in watercolour. It is used to protect white areas of the paper so that they do not get splashed with paint, or when you want the white of the paper to represent the lighter areas of your subject. Depending on the size and shape of the area you want to protect, masking fluid and masking tape are the most commonly used materials. Masking tape can also be used to secure heavy watercolour paper, which doesn't need to be stretched, to the drawing board.

Eraser ▲

A kneaded eraser is useful for correcting the pencil lines of your underdrawing, and for removing the lines so that they do not show through the paint on the finished painting.

Sponge ▲

Natural or synthetic sponges are useful for mopping up excess water. Small pieces of sponge can be used to lift off colour from wet paint. Sponges are also commonly used to apply paint, with the pitted surface of the sponge creating interesting textures on the paper.

Tips: • Store small painting accessories such as sponges and rolls of tape in lidded boxes to keep things neat and tidy; plastic food storage boxes are ideal.
• Store bottles upright and always put the lids back on immediately after use to prevent spillage.
• Wash sponges immediately after use.

From light to dark

One of the things that attracts people to watercolour painting, and the one characteristic for which watercolour is most renowned, is its translucency. Good watercolours glow with a light that seems to come from within the painting itself. The reason for this is that pure watercolour paints are transparent: when a wash of watercolour paint is applied to paper, the white of the paper shines through. This is what makes watercolour the perfect choice for capturing subtle nuances of light and shade and creating a feeling of airiness that is unrivalled by any other painting medium.

However, the transparency of the paint imposes a technical constraint that you need to be aware of. When one colour is laid on top of another, particles of the first colour will still show through.

In opaque media such as oils, you can obliterate a dark colour by placing a light one on top of it. In pure watercolour, however, if you try to paint a pale yellow on top of a dark blue, some of the blue will remain visible – so instead of yellow, the two colours will appear to merge to form a green.

In practical terms, this means that you have to work from light to dark, putting down the lightest tones first and working around them as you develop the painting. You have plan ahead and work out where the light tones and colours are going to be before you pick up a brush and begin the actual painting.

One other important consideration is that in pure (transparent) watercolour there is no such thing as white paint. If you want certain areas of your painting

to be white, the only white available to you is the white of the paper, and so you leave those areas free of paint, protecting them if necessary by applying some kind of mask. Alternatively, you can use white gouache, but gouache is opaque, and so you have to be very careful not to lose the feeling of luminosity.

Osprey ▼
The artist has combined watercolour with white gouache to great effect. The billowing clouds were created by leaving areas of the sky free of paint and by blotting off paint with a paper towel to soften the colour around the edges of the clouds. The ripples and spray in the water were painted using very dilute white gouache so as not to lose the wonderful feeling of light.

Stormy sky ▲

The artist began this study of a stormy sky by dampening the paper with clean water and dropping in a very pale grey colour, allowing it to spread of its own accord. She then blotted off paint in some areas with a paper towel to reveal the white of the paper before adding the mid- and dark greys and the deep blue of the sky, wet into wet.

Poppies ▶

Watercolour is a wonderful medium for painting translucent subjects such as flower petals. Following the light to dark rule, the artist began by putting down the very pale yellowy green colour that is visible in the background and around the edges of the flowers. She then gradually applied more layers of colour to build up the density of tone on the petals and make the flowers look three-dimensional, taking care to allow some of the first very pale washes to show through in places. Note how paint has been scraped off to create the striations in the petals and delineate the petal edges: using the white of the paper in this way adds "sparkle" to the image. Tiny touches of opaque yellow gouache give the flower centres and stems solidity, without destroying the translucency of the painting as a whole or the balance between the two media. Careful planning and observation of the light and dark tones have resulted in a fresh and spontaneous-looking study of a perennially popular subject.

Making marks

Although artists are, by definition, inventive and apply watercolour paint with a variety of tools in order to create as wide a range of marks as possible, a brush is still the most basic and the best tool for the job. There are so many different brushes on the market that it seems as if there is a shape and a size to cover every eventuality, and it is easy to get carried away and buy a lot of brushes that you will rarely, if ever, use. With a little practice, however, you will find that you can get a remarkable range and variety of marks from a single, carefully chosen brush simply by altering the way you hold it and apply it to the paper.

A good first brush is a round, soft-haired (preferably sable) watercolour brush. This is probably the most widely used and versatile type. A medium round brush (say, no.8 or no.10) is a good, general-purpose brush, as it holds sufficient paint to make washes but also comes to a good point for fine detail work.

The conventional, and perhaps the most obvious, way to hold a brush is to hold it in the same way as you would a pen or a pencil, but that is by no means the only option.

Holding the brush with four fingers on one side of the barrel and your thumb on the other and pushing or pulling it quickly sideways will leave a broken smear of paint that is perfect for depicting texture and is totally unlike the mark made when using the point of the brush. These marks can be long or short; the density and spread of paint depends on the speed of the stroke.

Holding the brush vertically allows you to make a stabbing action, which results in a series of individual marks. You can vary the size of the marks by altering the amount of pressure you apply and the speed at which you apply it. The amount of pressure that you apply also has a marked effect. Increasing the amount of pressure that you apply, so that more of the sable hair comes into contact with the support, increases the width of the stroke.

A flat or a mop-shaped brush will result in a completely different range of marks. Experiment with different brushes to find out what you can achieve.

Strokes of an even width
To create strokes of an even width, use the tip of the brush and apply a steady pressure. Apply more pressure to increase the width of the line. For short strokes, you may find it helpful to rest your little finger on the paper surface as a balance, but take care not to smudge any wet paint if you do this.

Dots
A stabbing or stippling creates a series of dots or blob-shaped marks. Holding the brush in an upright position helps to speed up the process and make it more controllable.

Strokes of varying widths
Varying the amount of pressure you apply also varies the width of the brushstroke, resulting in expressive calligraphic marks.

Broad washes
To make a wash that covers a wide area, use the side of the brush, rather than the point, and apply even pressure as you make the stroke.

> **Tip**: Load your brush with plenty of paint. Using too little paint will mean that you run out quickly, often in mid mark. The amount of paint delivered to the support should come as much from the pressure applied as from the amount of liquid held within the brush fibres.

Brush shape

Pressing the brush to the paper surface without moving it results in marks that reflect the shapes of the brush.

Thick and thin

Provided your brush holds a point well, you can create marks that vary greatly in thickness by applying more or less pressure.

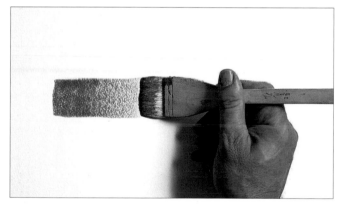

Quick washes

A Japanese-style hake brush holds a large amount of paint, and this makes it easy to lay flat washes. This is a good choice of brush if you need to cover a large area with paint.

Thin lines

Used on its edge and with a light touch, even a large flat brush can be made to make delicate brush marks. Practise until you get a feel for the amount of pressure needed.

Uniform pattern

Using even pressure and the corner of the brush to dab or stipple paint on to the support will result in a series of uniformly shaped marks.

Varying the texture

Using a similar stippling action while varying the pressure and the angle at which the brush is held will create a loosely textured area, made up of marks of different shapes.

Washes

A wash is the term used to describe the process of applying watercolour paint in a single layer. There are three kinds of washes – flat, gradated and variegated (which is really a variation on a gradated wash). Although the technique is broadly the same way in all three cases, the results look very different.

Washes are among the most fundamental of all watercolour techniques. Sometimes washes are applied over the whole of the paper, and sometimes they are used over only selected areas. It is very rare for a painting to be composed entirely of washes, but as a wash of one kind or another is very often the first stage in producing a watercolour, it is well worth taking the time and trouble to master the technique. It will stand you in good stead for all your subsequent work and is an essential first step in getting used to manipulating paint on paper.

A flat wash is, as the name implies, a wash that is completely even in tone. All pictures need some blank and uncluttered areas, so flat washes are necessary on occasions, either to provide a base for the rest of the painting or as "breathing spaces" that allow the viewer's eye to rest. Flat washes can be particularly useful in abstract, or semi-abstract, work. In representational work, however, too many flat washes will lead to a dull and uninteresting painting. A flat wash contrasts well with many of the techniques used to introduce texture into watercolour paintings, such as spattering and stippling, as well as with other media, such as pastels, inks and coloured pencils.

Gradated and variegated washes are both designed to give some variety of tone. Like the flat wash, both are normally used in conjunction with other techniques. Both gradated and variegated washes are particularly useful in landscape painting.

> **Tip**: It is difficult to mix two washes that are identical in tone, so always mix more wash than you think you will need, so that you don't have to stop halfway through a painting to mix more, then find that you cannot match the tone.

Flat wash

A well laid flat wash should show no variation in tone. Having said that, however, the kind of paper you use does have an effect and it is worth experimenting so that you know what results you can expect.

Work smoothly and confidently, without hesitation. Never go back over an area that you have already painted or the tones will be uneven. Work with your drawing board flat, or angle it slightly to help the paint flow down the paper. Use a large round-headed brush that holds a lot of paint, so that you can work quickly without having to re-load the brush.

1 Using a large wash brush, mix a generous amount of wash (here, sap green was used). Working from left to right, lay a smooth stroke of colour across the paper.

2 Quickly re-load your brush with more paint. Pick up the pool of paint at the base of the first stroke with your brush and continue across the paper, again working from left to right.

3 If you find you've got too much paint at the base of the wash, dry your brush on tissue paper and run it along the base of the wash to pick up the uneven streaks.

The finished flat wash
The wash has dried to a flat, even tone with no variation or visible brushstrokes.

The fewer strokes you use, the flatter the wash will be – so use a large brush if you want to cover the whole paper.

Gradated wash

A gradated wash is painted in a similar way to a flat wash, using a large brush and brushstrokes that dry evenly without leaving any streaks, but it shows a variation in tone. More water is added to the wash as you work down the paper so that the colour gradually gets lighter. Alternatively, you can add more pigment to the wash so that it gradually becomes darker in tone.

A gradated wash is often used to paint skies which, because of the effects of aerial perspective, are usually darkest at the top of the painting and paler towards the horizon.

You can also use a gradated wash to make one side of your subject darker in tone than another; the dark side looks as if it is in shadow, and this helps to make your subject look three-dimensional. Transitional gradations such as this are excellent for painting curved surfaces, such as glass bottles, oranges and domed roofs.

1 Lay the first stroke of colour as for a flat wash, working from left to right with smooth, even strokes.

2 Add more water to the wash to make a paler tone and continue to work across the page from left to right.

3 Continue as before, adding more water to the wash with each stroke so that it gets lighter as you move down.

4 As more water is added to the paint mixture, the colour virtually disappears.

The finished gradated wash

In the final wash, the colour has paled from a strong tone at the top to almost nothing at the base.

Practice exercise: **Landscape using flat and gradated washes**

Although washes are among the most fundamental of watercolour techniques, they can be used as the basis for simple little studies that you can be proud to hang on your wall.

This exercise is based around using flat and gradated washes to establish the planes of an imaginary landscape scene. The simple detailing that is added on top of the washes – the trees and the distant farmhouse – create texture and add visual interest to the painting.

You could easily adapt this exercise to create an imaginary landscape of your own. Choose colours for the underlying washes that are appropriate to the main subject of the painting – perhaps warm yellows and greens for a woodland scene, or blues for a seascape.

Materials
- *2B pencil*
- *140lb (300gsm) rough watercolour paper, pre-stretched*
- *Watercolour paints: cerulean blue, yellow ochre, cadmium lemon, cobalt blue, viridian, raw sienna, Payne's grey, ultramarine violet, neutral tint, light red, cadmium red, burnt umber*
- *Brushes: large mop, medium round, fine round*

Reference sketch
A quick sketch made in situ outdoors, when standing in front of your chosen scene, is a useful way of trying out compositions and colour combinations to see what works best. Use it as reference material to produce a more detailed painting when you get home.

1 Using a 2B pencil, sketch the main shapes of the subject – in this case, the foreground path, the house and trees in the middle distance, and the tree-covered hills in the background.

3 At the bottom of the gradated wash, where the colour has paled to almost nothing, put down a broad stroke of very pale yellow ochre. You may need to tilt the drawing board backwards slightly to prevent paint from flowing into the dry part of the paper, below the sky area.

2 Using a large mop brush, dampen the whole of the sky area with clean water. As soon as you have finished, lay a gradated wash of cerulean blue across the top of the sky.

4 While the first wash is still damp, lay a stroke of cerulean blue across the top of the sky to intensify the colour. Leave to dry. Mix a pale green from cadmium lemon and cerulean blue and wash it over the foreground grass on either side of the road and the trees in the middle distance. Leave to dry.

5 Mix a bluish green from cobalt blue and a little viridian. Using a large mop brush, wash the paint over the tree-covered hill in the distance, taking care to leave the house untouched. You may need to use a finer brush to go around the outline of the house. Dot in the shapes of trees along the horizon and leave to dry.

6 Mix an olive green from raw sienna, cobalt blue and a little cadmium lemon. Brush the mixture over the trees and the foreground. Mix a pale mauve from Payne's grey and ultramarine violet and paint the road. Leave to dry.

7 Mix a dark green from neutral tint and viridian. Using a medium round brush, paint in the dark shapes of the trees. Don't worry too much about making the shapes accurate, just go for the overall effect. Leave to dry.

8 Mix a strong wash of ultramarine violet and paint a broad stroke of colour below the trees, to the right of the farmhouse. Paint another to the left of the road to indicate the brightly coloured fields of lavender.

9 Paint the roofs in light red and the outline of the road sign in cadmium red. Note how these small touches of hot colour stand out against the cool blues and greens used elsewhere in the painting. Mix a wash of ultramarine violet and burnt umber, and paint over the foreground road.

10 Mix a warm brown from cadmium lemon, raw sienna and a little cobalt blue. Paint in the fine foreground grasses, using a fine round brush.

The finished painting

This painting effectively combines flat and gradated washes in a charming landscape that is full of character. Flat washes of colour on the hillside and winding foreground road, and a gradated wash of cerulean blue on the sky, establish the basis of the scene, while a few simple details – the broad strokes of colour for the trees in the distance, the sharp lines of the foreground grasses and the small touches of red on the roof in the middle distance – help to bring the scene to life.

Variegated wash on damp paper

A variegated wash is a variation on the gradated wash, but instead of adding more water, you gradually introduce another colour. When properly done, the transition from one colour to the next should be almost imperceptible.

Some artists find it easier to dampen the paper first, using either a sponge or a lmop brush dipped in clean water. This allows the colours to blend and merge in a much more subtle way, without any risk of hard lines appearing between one colour and the next. You may need to allow the paper to dry slightly before you apply any paint: this is something you will learn with practice. However, if you prefer, you can work on dry paper.

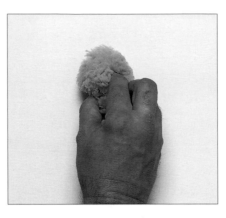

1 Dampen the paper with a sponge dipped in clean water. Use plenty of water: you can let the paper dry a little before applying the paint, if necessary.

2 Using a large wash brush, lay a stroke of colour over the paper, working from left to right. The paint spreads more evenly on damp paper.

3 Clean your brush thoroughly and load it with a second colour. Start laying this colour over the first. Continue until the wash is complete.

Variegated wash on damp paper
In the finished wash, the colours merge together almost imperceptibly, with no obvious division between the two.

Variegated wash on dry paper
Here, the division between the two colours is slightly more obvious.

Practice exercise: **Sunset using a variegated wash**

A variegated wash is one of the most useful techniques for painting a sunset in watercolour. This simple exercise also shows you how to create a silhouette to turn the variegated wash into an attractive landscape painting.

Materials
- 2B pencil
- 140lb (300gsm) rough watercolour paper, pre-stretched
- Watercolour paints: ultramarine blue, cadmium orange, cadmium red, ultramarine violet, alizarin crimson, sepia
- Brushes: large round, small round

The original scene
Striking colours, shimmering reflections and a bold silhouette – all the ingredients for a sunset with impact.

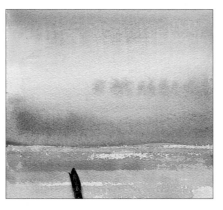

1 Using a 2B pencil, lightly sketch the outline of the silhouetted trees on the skyline. Using a large round brush, dampen the paper with clean water. Mix a wash of ultramarine blue and, again using the large round brush, lay a gradated wash over the top half of the paper, adding more water with each brushstroke so that the blue colour pales to almost nothing just above the horizon.

2 Mix an orangey red from cadmium orange and cadmium red. While the paper is still damp lay this colour over the lower half of the paper, allowing it to merge wet into wet into the very pale blue around the horizon line. Leave to dry. Dampen the paper again very slightly. Brush a broad stroke of the same orangey red mix across the middle of the painting (this will form the basis of the silhouetted land area) and dot it into the sky. Leave to dry.

3 Mix a warm purple from ultramarine violet and a little alizarin crimson. Using a large round brush, brush this mixture on to the sky to represent the dark cloud shapes. Add a little more pigment to the mixture to make a darker tone and paint the outline of the silhouetted trees. Using the same mixture, paint a few broken brushstrokes on the water for the dark reflections of both the trees and the land area.

4 Mix a dark violet from ultramarine violet and sepia and darken the silhouetted area, adding a few fine vertical lines for the boat masts that stick up into the sky.

The finished painting

A two-colour variegated wash forms the basis of this colourful sunset, while a bold silhouette gives the viewer a strong shape on which to focus. Although the painting itself is very simple, the choice of rich colours and the careful placing of both the silhouetted land form and the reflections in the water combine to make an atmospheric little study.

The initial blue wash merges almost imperceptibly with the rich, warm colours of the sunset.

The white of the paper shows through in places – a simple but effective way of implying water sparkling in the last rays of the setting sun.

Understanding tone

"Tone" is a word that you will often come across in art books: it simply means the relative lightness or darkness of a colour. The exact tone depends on the degree and quality of light falling on a particular object: if one side of an object is in shadow, it will be darker in tone than a side that is in direct sunlight. You can often see this clearly by looking at two adjacent sides of a building, where the front of the building is illuminated by the sun and the other forms one side of a narrow, shaded alleyway. Both sides of the building are made from the same materials, and we know they are the same colour, but the side that is in shade looks considerably darker.

But why is tone important in painting? The answer is that it enables you to create a convincing impression of light and shade, and this is one of the things that helps to make your subjects look three-dimensional.

This means that you have to analyse your subject and decide at the outset where the lightest areas of your painting are going to be. Because watercolour paint is transparent and you cannot lay a light colour on top of a dark one without the underlying colour showing through, you usually start with the lightest tones and build up to the darkest. Before you begin painting, therefore, it is often helpful to make a quick tonal sketch to work out where the light, medium and dark tones should be placed. Get the tonal structure right and much of the rest of your work will fall into place.

Single-colour subject ▼

Even a single-colour subject, such as this strongly lit orange, consists of hundreds of slightly different tones. The human eye, however, can only make out the difference between a fraction of this number.

Tonal sketch ▼

When you sketch a single-colour subject, you need to show some differences in tone in order for it to look convincing. However, most images will still read convincingly when broken into only a handful of tones, as here. The side of the orange

that faces away from the light, looks dark. The side that is directly illuminated by the light is a much lighter tone. In very strong light, the best way to convey this may be to leave highlight areas completely white and untouched by paint.

Translating colours to tones

But just how do you analyse the tones in your subject? We're used to describing things by their colour – red, blue, green and so on – but assessing tones is a different matter. One of the best ways to grasp the concept is try to imagine what a black-and-white photograph of your subject would look like.

Confusingly, colours that look very different (say, red and green) may turn out to be very similar in tone, while colours that you might expect to be light in tone (such as yellow) may actually be fairly dark, depending on how the light hits them. In addition, of course, you will find infinitely subtle gradations of tone across an object.

To make it simple, break down what you see into a few tones only – say, four or five – varying from white to black in stages. To get yourself more attuned to tones, set up some contrasting objects and, using numbers, place them in the correct order from light to dark. Time yourself. You will gradually train yourself to recognize tones more quickly. Start with objects that are strongly lit from one side, as this makes it easier to discern different tones, and gradually move on to more evenly lit objects as you develop your ability to assess tonal values. Another useful exercise is to make black-and-white photocopies of colour photographs.

Multi-coloured subject ▲
When you're dealing with a subject that contains many colours, it can be difficult to work out which tones are light and which ones are dark. Try to imagine your subject as if it was a black-and-white photograph.

Colour converted to tone ▲
Note that different colours – for example, the oranges and the foreground lemon – are very similar in tone. The shaded sides of the bananas, which we know to be a lighter yellow than the lemon, look darker than one might expect.

Mixing tones

Once you've trained yourself to analyse tones, you need to apply this knowledge in your paintings. In pure watercolour, you make tones darker by adding more pigment (or black) and lighter by adding more water. Practise doing this with a range of different colours so that you get better at judging how much more pigment or water to add.

Tonal strip ▼
Here, alizarin crimson watercolour paint (shown in the centre of the strip) has been progressively darkened by adding black and lightened by adding water.

▶

Practice exercise: **Tonal study in monochrome**

This exercise trains you to assess tone by using five tones of the same colour to create a three-dimensional impression of blue and green children's play bricks. The image is painted in layers, working from light to dark, with each layer being allowed to dry before the next one is applied.

Note that the tone of the mixed washes always looks darker when it is wet than it does when it is dry. With practice you will learn to compensate for this by mixing your tones so that, when you first apply them, they appear to be a little darker or more intense than necessary.

Once you have done this exercise, try your own versions of it using other objects that you might have lying around the home. Books and plastic food containers are good choices as they are straight sided, so you can concentrate on the tones without having to worry too much about getting the shapes right.

Materials
- *200lb (425gsm) NOT watercolour paper, pre-stretched*
- *2B pencil*
- *Watercolour pigment: burnt umber*
- *Brush: medium round*

The set-up
Set up your subject on a plain white background (a large sheet of paper will do), with a table lamp in front and slightly to the left of it. Spend some time looking at it in order to decide which tone each area is going to be. If it helps, make a quick pencil sketch and number each area from one to five, with one being the lightest tone and five the darkest.

1 Using a 2B pencil, lightly sketch the bricks, taking careful note of where they overlap. Mix a thin wash of burnt umber (tone 1) and, using a medium round brush, paint all the brick shapes in this tone. This is the lightest tone.

2 Strengthen the wash slightly by adding a little more burnt umber pigment (tone 2). Leaving the lightest area (the side of the green brick) untouched, apply tone 2 over all the remaining areas. Even though only two tones have been used so far, the image instantly begins to have form.

3 Add a little more pigment to the wash to darken it further and brush it over those areas that are in deeper shadow (tone 3). The shape of the three bricks is becoming ever more apparent. The tone is deepened both by adding more pigment and by overlaying successive layers of colour.

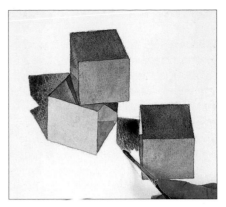

4 Now mix up tone 4. As before, do not by make a new mix, but instead, add more burnt umber pigment to the previous one to make it darker. Carefully apply this tone along the lower edge of, and below, the topmost blue brick, where a small shadow is cast across the green brick.

5 Tone 5, the darkest tone (created by the deep shadow reflected in the slightly shiny surface), is evident on the left-hand side of the topmost brick. A similar dark tone can be seen on the right-hand side of the brick below. This is created by the reflection of the shadow from the right-hand brick.

6 Put the finishing touches to the study by adding the cast shadow of all three bricks. Leave to dry.

The finished painting

Although this is nothing more than a technical exercise, the bricks look convincingly three-dimensional. This is entirely due to the fact that the artist paid very careful attention to the relative tones and built up the density by overlaying several layers where necessary, even though he used only five tones of the same colour to make the painting.

The darker tones are created by adding more pigment to the wash and also by applying several layers so that the tone is darkened gradually.

The lightest tone is created by means of a single wash of tone 1.

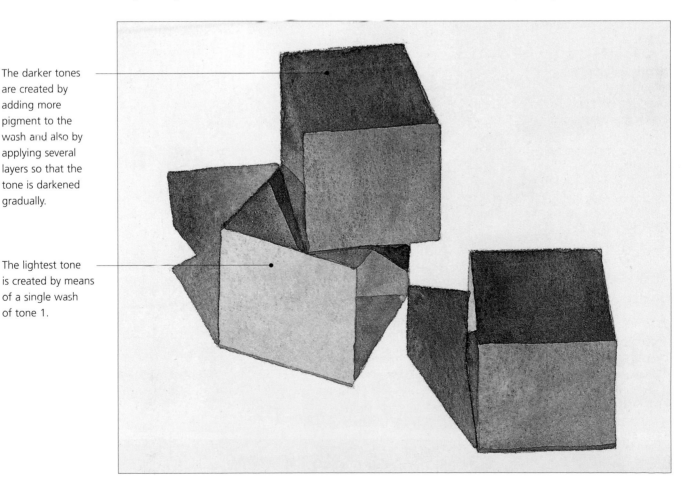

Understanding colour

Colour is an important element in most artistic endeavours, but in order to capture the subtle and elusive qualities of light seen in the best watercolours, a basic knowledge of colour theory is especially valuable. It will help you to understand why some colour mixes work better than others, and how to use the emotional effect of colours in your paintings.

Primary, secondary and tertiary colours

It was the Englishman Isaac Newton who first proved that white light is made by the mixing together of the seven spectrum colours of red, orange, yellow, green, blue, indigo (or blue/violet), and violet. This is known as additive colour mixing, because the "adding" together of the seven spectrum colours results in white light.

Pigment colours, however, behave in a different way. Mix together a similar range of pigment colours and the result is an almost black, mud-coloured mess. This is because every time you mix one pigment colour with another, the resulting colour is always duller and less pure than the parent colours. The more colours that are mixed together, the less pure the resulting colour will be, and the darker the resulting mix. If the three primary colours are mixed together, all the light waves are absorbed from white light, ultimately resulting in black. In other words, you subtract light and so this is known as subtractive colour mixing.

The classic diagram for explaining colour theory is the colour wheel, which illustrates the relationships between the different colours. Red, yellow and blue are the three primary pigment colours. These can only be manufactured: they cannot be mixed by combining any other colours. They are also sometimes known as the "first" or "principal" colours.

Mixing equal amounts of red with yellow creates a mid-orange; mixing yellow with blue creates a mid-green; and mixing blue with red creates a mid-violet. These are known as the secondary colours.

Mixing a primary colour with an equal amount of the secondary colour next to it results in six more colours, which are known as tertiary colours. These are red-orange, orange-yellow, yellow-green, green-blue, blue-violet, and violet-red. The quality and intensity of these tertiary colours can be extended almost indefinitely, not only by varying the proportion of the primary and secondary colours used in the mix, but also by varying the amount of water added to lighten them.

However, it is important to remember that there are many different versions of the three primary colours, and your choice of primaries therefore dictates the kind of secondary and tertiary colours that you can mix.

Warm colour wheel ▶
This colour wheel shows the secondary and tertiary mixes that are made using the classic warm primaries of cadmium red, cadmium yellow and ultramarine blue.

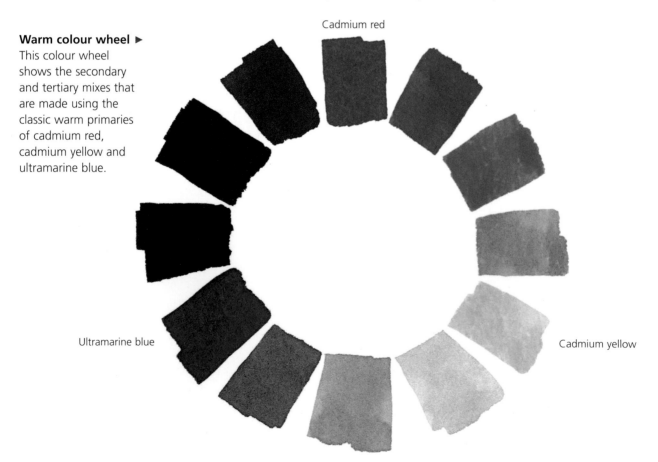

Cadmium red

Ultramarine blue

Cadmium yellow

Cool colour wheel ▶
This colour wheel shows the secondary and tertiary colour mixes that are made using the classic "cool" primaries of alizarin crimson, cadmium lemon and cerulean blue.

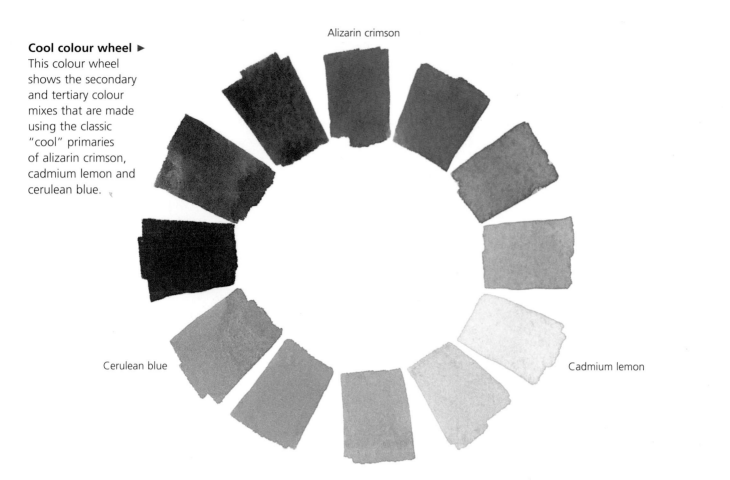

Alizarin crimson

Cerulean blue

Cadmium lemon

The language of colour

There are several terms relating to colour that you may come across in art books and magazines. It is important to be clear about the meaning of each.

A hue is simply another name for a colour. Red, purple and yellow are all hues. Two different reds might be described as being close in hue, while yellow and blue are different hues. There are many different versions (or hues) of the primary reds, yellows and blues, and the quality of the secondary and tertiary colour mixes depends very much on which of the primary versions you use.

A tint is made when white is added to a colour, or, in the case of pure watercolour, clean water. The opposite of a tint is a shade. This is made by making the colour darker, either by adding black or a little of its complementary colour. When you make a shade, the colour should not change dramatically in hue.

Mixing from different primaries ▶
The primary phthalocyanine blue is mixed with two versions of primary red, cadmium red (left) and alizarin crimson (right), to create two different violets.

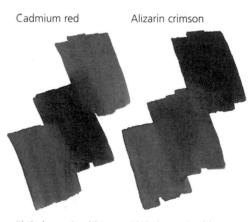

Cadmium red   Alizarin crimson

Phthalocyanine blue   Phthalocyanine blue

Shades ◀——————————— Hue ———————————▶ Tints

Colour temperature

All colours are described as being either warm or cool. We think of red, orange and yellow as being warm colours; these are found on one side of the colour wheel, opposite the so-called cool colours of violet, blue and green. However all colours, regardless of their position on the colour wheel, have either a warm or a cool bias. For example, blue is a cool colour and red is a warm colour, but you can have a warm blue or a cool red. If a red has a blue bias, it is described as cool; if a red has a yellow bias, it is described as warm.

In order to be able to mix a full range of colours, you need to include both warm and cool variants of at least the three primaries in your chosen palette.

Warm and cool primaries ▶
This illustration shows the classic warm primaries (top row) and the classic cool primaries (bottom row).

Cadmium red

Cadmium yellow

Ultramarine blue

Alizarin crimson

Cadmium lemon

Cerulean blue

Modern paint technology, however, has meant that paint manufacturers now have primary reds, blues, and yellows that display very little or no warm or cool bias. These are the perfect primaries which, in theory, make it possible to mix a full range of colours from just three.

Colour temperature is an important part of colour mixing. Those primary colours that have a bias towards one another on the colour wheel invariably make more intense secondaries when mixed. Primaries that lean away from each other result in muted secondaries.

Colour temperature is especially important when you are trying to create the illusion of depth. Warm colours are perceived to advance while cool ones recede, so objects painted in a warm colour seem to be closer to the viewer.

Intense and subdued secondary mixes ▶
Secondary and tertiary mixes are either intense or subdued, depending on the primary hues used to create them.

Here, ultramarine blue, which has a red bias, is mixed with cadmium yellow, which also has a red bias. This places them further apart on the colour wheel and results in a subdued secondary.

Phthalocyanine blue, on the other hand, has a yellow bias, and this results in an intense secondary when mixed with cadmium lemon.

Subdued secondary

Intense secondary

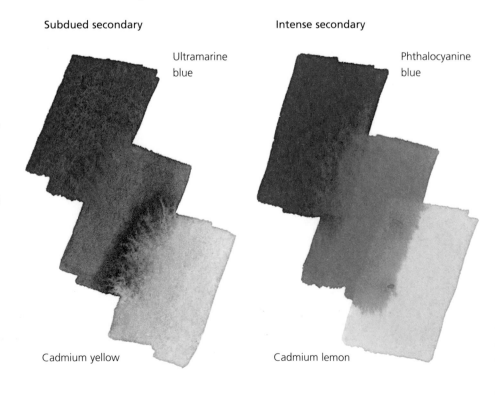

Ultramarine blue

Phthalocyanine blue

Cadmium yellow

Cadmium lemon

Colour contrast

Colours that fall opposite each other across the colour wheel – such as orange/blue, yellow/violet and red/green – have a special relationship and are known as complementary pairs. When they are placed next to each other in a painting, complementary colours create vibrant colour contrasts and have the effect of making each other appear more intense than they really are.

This is due to an effect known as "simultaneous contrast". If you stare at an area of green and then look away to a white surface, you will see a red after-image – red being the complementary of green. If red is placed next to a green area, it will be visually intensified by this red after-image. Likewise, the green would be intensified by the green after-image from the red. This effect can be used to add intensity to your work.

Complementary pairs ▶
These special colour pairings seem more intense when placed next to each other, but they neutralize each other when the paints are physically mixed together.

Orange and blue   Yellow and violet   Red and green

Mixing complementaries

If a little of one complementary colour is added to another, it subdues the recipient colour, knocking it back but without dulling it in the way that adding black would. If more of the colour's complementary is added, the result (depending on which complementaries are used) is a range of browns and greys, known as neutral colours. The advantage of mixing neutral colours in this way, rather than by adding black, is that the mixes look much fresher.

If you look at a colour wheel, you will see that regardless of their position all complementary pairs are, to a greater or lesser extent, composed of all three primary colours. When you mix equal amounts of all three primaries together, the result is a dark grey – almost black. However, by carefully managing the relative amounts of the three primaries that enter the mix, you can create a wonderful range of subtle, neutral mixes that echo those found in the natural world.

Mixing neutral greys ▼
Neutral greys and browns are made by mixing together two complementary colours. Here, progressively larger amounts of viridian green are added to alizarin crimson, resulting in a dark grey. A range of grey tints is then made by adding increasing amounts of water.

Colour harmony

Using harmonious colours that work well together creates a distinct feel or mood, and this adds immeasurably to the success of a work. This is especially true if you are trying to depict a specific season of the year or time of day, or if you are trying to show how a subject has been lit, for example, a still life bathed in candlelight or a figure lit with harsh mid-day light.

As the colour wheel below shows, there are many different ways of achieving colour harmony. With practice you will find that your instinct is the best guide: if something looks right, then it is right. However, a little basic theory about colour harmony will set you on the right path.

Different types of colour harmony ▼
Complementary harmony is created by using those colours that fall opposite each other on the colour wheel. Triad harmony is achieved by using the colours found at the angles of an equilateral triangle, superimposed at any position over the colour wheel. Using an isosceles triangle will point to the colours to form a split complementary, while using a square or a rectangle will produce tetrad harmonies. Alternatively, you can create harmony by using those colours that have one primary in common or are close to each other on the colour wheel. These are known as analogous colours.

Tone and optical mixing

Traditional watercolour technique relies on one transparent wash being laid over another in such a way as to modify or consolidate the initial wash without necessarily obliterating it. It is, however, easy to overdo these wash layers so that the image and the colours look dull, lacking the sparkle and elusive inner light for which good watercolour is renowned.

Try to think ahead when planning your work, and aim to use no more than three layers of wash at the most. Working on the light to dark principle, the first washes would include the lightest tones and colours, the second layer the mid-tones and colours, and the final layer the darkest ones. As with all best laid plans, of course, this is not always possible, but it is a useful discipline to keep in mind. This is one of the reasons why the ability to assess tonal values is such an important part of watercolour painting.

Building up colour density ▼
Colour density can be built up by overlaying washes. This illustration shows three layers of the same colour, though the same principle holds true when you apply different colours on top of each other.

This layering technique can also create colour mixes that are impossible when certain colours are mixed together physically. Physically mixing any two complementary colours together will result in the chosen colours being neutralized and, depending on the amounts used, being turned into a brown or a grey. However, you can mix these colours optically by applying a transparent wash of one colour over a dry wash of the other. This retains the integrity of both washes; a certain amount of the lower wash colour will show through the upper wash, modifying it. Another name for this type of colour application is broken colour. It can provide both texture and interest to those areas of a work where the colour is intrinsically flat and featureless, as well as being used to depict difficult subjects consisting of complex colour variations, such as foliage, water or extreme weather conditions.

Optical mixes ▼
When one wash is applied over another, wet on dry, the two colours mix optically to produce a third colour. These optical mixes look crisp and clean, as the colours retain their integrity.

Physical mixes ▼
When colours are mixed physically, the resulting colours look duller than their optical counterparts. This is true regardless of whether the colours are mixed wet into wet (left) or wet on dry.

Practice exercise: **Overlaying colours**

In this exercise, colours are overlaid both to build up density of tone and to optically "mix" colours on the paper. Because watercolour paint is transparent, some of the colour of your initial wash will show through any subsequent washes, modifying their appearance. The only way you can be sure of the effect is to practise on a piece of scrap paper in advance. Remember that watercolour always looks lighter when it is dry, so you must wait until your practice piece is completely dry before deciding whether you've got the colour you want.

Materials
- *140lb (300gsm) NOT watercolour paper, pre-stretched*
- *2B pencil*
- *Watercolour paints: cerulean blue, lemon yellow, yellow ochre, burnt umber, mauve, alizarin crimson, cadmium yellow*
- *Brushes: large round, fine round, mop*
- *Sponge*

The set-up
When setting up a still life, choose objects of different shapes and sizes. The elongated shape of the pear and the rounded swede (rutabaga) used here give interesting visual contrasts. In terms of their colour, the same underlying green occurs on both, giving unity to the still life, while the red coloration on the swede complements the green, making it more exciting.

1 Lightly sketch the pear and swede. Mix a bright green from cerulean blue and lemon yellow, and brush over the pear, leaving highlights untouched. Dot paint on to give an uneven texture.

Tip: When drawing fruit, work out the position of the stem and the base and draw a line between them to help get the angle of the fruit right.

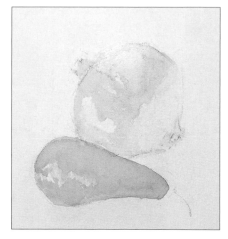

2 Add more cerulean blue to the mixture and more water to make it very dilute, and brush it unevenly over the top half of the swede, again leaving some gaps. You have now established the underlying colours of both the pear and the swede. These colours will be allowed to show through in parts of the finished painting, but they will also influence any colours that are laid down on top of them, creating mixes that could not be achieved in the palette.

3 Mix a dark brown from yellow ochre, a little burnt umber and a touch of mauve. Using the side of the brush, brush this mixture unevenly over the pear, leaving gaps in places so that some of the first green wash is visible. The brown mixture is transparent, hence its appearance is modified by the underlying bright green. The two colours on top of each other look like a dull, mottled green.

4 Mix a dull purple from mauve with a little burnt umber and brush it over the swede, making the top lighter than the bottom by adding more water. As on the pear, keep the texture and density of tone uneven by dotting more paint on in places. While the paint is still wet, build up the colour by touching more paint into selected areas so that it spreads wet into wet and you do not get any hard-edged shapes.

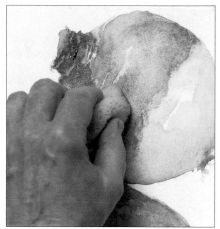

5 Mix a dilute wash of yellow ochre and brush it over the lower half of the swede, adding more pigment as you work down so that the base is darker. While the paint is still wet, brush a line of the green used in Step 1 between the two halves of the swede.

6 Using the same mixture as before, continue building up tone and depth on the purple half of the swede, applying the paint unevenly to create interesting textures. Using the same dark brown mixture as in Step 3, put a few spots and blemishes on the pear.

7 Mix up a very dilute wash of alizarin crimson. Using a small sponge, dab it on to the purple half of the swede. Crimson and green are complementary colours, so using the two together in the picture immediately gives it a lift. Leave to dry.

8 Mix a warm orange from alizarin crimson and cadmium yellow. Using a large mop brush, brush this mixture carefully on to the background; you may need to tilt the board to prevent paint from running over the pear or swede. Mix a dark brown from burnt umber and mauve and, using a fine round brush, paint the pear stem.

The finished painting
The initial green washes have modified the colour of subsequent layers, creating subtle optical mixes that are more effective than a single, solid wash could ever be. Applying several layers of the same colour (as on the swede) allows you to build up the tone gradually.

The shadows under the pear and swede anchor them to the surface and make the still life look more three-dimensional.

The "woodgrain" is painted using a more pigmented version of the background colour plus a little mauve.

The background colour harmonizes with the pear and swede but is sufficiently different to allow them to stand out.

Wet into wet

Working wet into wet means exactly what it says – applying wet paint to wetted paper. When you do this, the paint spreads outwards in soft-edged blurs, and the wetter the paper, the further the paint spreads. You can apply paint either to paper that has been dampened with clean water or on top of a wash that has not yet dried, creating interesting colour mixes. Paint will not spread into any areas that are completely dry.

Dropping gorgeous, rich colours on to wetted paper is an exhilarating experience, as you can never predict exactly what will happen or how far the paint will spread on the paper. For many people, that unpredictability is part of the charm of watercolour painting.

Colours that have been applied wet into wet always look lighter when they dry than they do when they are first put on. With experience you will learn to compensate for this by using stronger, more pigmented washes.

The wet-into-wet technique is excellent for cloudy skies, distant trees and woods, and atmospheric effects, such as fogs or storms. However, a picture painted entirely wet into wet would look very blurred and indistinct. Try to keep a balance between wet-into-wet areas and sharper, more clearly defined sections. It is particularly important not to make the foreground too blurred. The soft-focus effect of wet into wet is normally best reserved for distant parts of a scene where you do not want a lot of sharp detail. When you apply paint on top of wet-into-wet washes that have dried, make sure you allow the underlying, diffuse effect of wet into wet to be seen in places, otherwise you will lose the character of the technique.

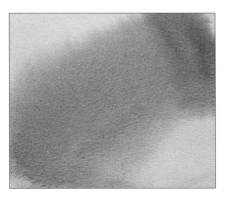

On very damp paper ▲
The paint spreads far beyond the line of the brushstroke.

On moderately damp paper ▲
The paint still blurs but it does not spread so far.

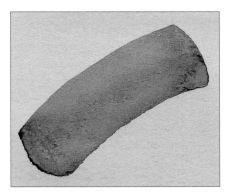

On almost dry paper ▲
The paint barely spreads beyond the brushstroke.

Practice exercise: **Still life painted wet into wet**

With their wonderful markings and silvery undersides, mackerel are beautiful fish to paint. This exercise allows you to practise controlling the degree of wetness on the paper. On the background and undersides of the fish, paint is applied to very damp paper so that it spreads freely. For the markings, the paint is applied to paper that is only very slightly damp. The paint blurs a little but the markings remain distinct.

Materials
- *2B pencil*
- *140lb (300gsm) rough watercolour paper, pre-stretched*
- *Watercolour paints: Payne's grey, Delft blue, alizarin crimson, aureolin, viridian, raw sienna, light red, sap green, cadmium lemon*
- *Brushes: large round*

The set-up
Crumpled brown parcel paper provides a textured but simple background to this still life. Arrange the fish so that you can see both the markings and the silvery belly, and add a lemon for a touch of extra colour. Position a lamp to one side of your subject, so that it casts definite shadows.

1 Using a 2B pencil, lightly sketch the still life. Using a large round brush, dampen the fish with clean water, leaving the highlights around the eyes and on the belly untouched and keeping within the outline of the fish. Mix a greyish blue from Payne's grey and Delft blue. Brush this mixture on to the damp areas so that it spreads.

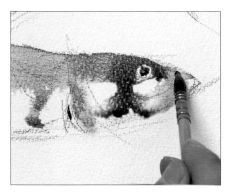

2 Add a little more Delft blue to the mixture and, using the tip of the brush, touch in the dark details around the head, again working carefully around the highlight areas.

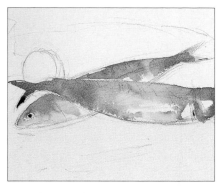

3 While the first wash is still damp, brush alizarin crimson on to the belly of the foreground fish and the head of the background fish. It will merge with the underlying wash. Leave to dry.

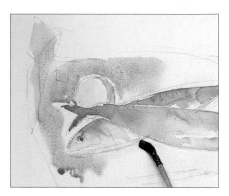

4 Dampen the lemon and brush on a pale mix of aureolin. Mix a pale green and brush on to the shaded side of the lemon. Leave to dry. Dampen the background and brush on raw sienna.

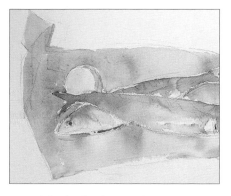

5 While the background wash is still damp, add a little light red to the raw sienna and touch it into those areas of the background that you want to appear darkest in order to build up the tone and imply the creases in the paper. Leave to dry.

6 Mix a dark blue-grey from Delft blue, Payne's grey and a little alizarin crimson. Dampen the backs of the fish with clean water and brush the paint on to the darkest areas. Add more Delft blue to the mixture and, when the paper is nearly dry, paint the markings.

7 Dampen the darkest areas of the background and touch in more of the mixture used in Step 5. Paint the lemon segments in aureolin. Dampen the rest of the lemon and brush a mixture of sap green and cadmium lemon on to the right-hand side.

The finished painting
The subtle transitions of colour on the bellies of the fish and the background paper could only be achieved using the wet-into-wet technique. These areas contrast well with the dry applications of colour on the lemon and around the fish head.

Several layers of colour are applied to the background while the paper is still very damp. The paint spreads, creating soft-edged blocks of colour.

For the markings, the paint is applied to paper that is only slightly damp. It spreads enough to soften the markings, but not so far that they become blurred and indistinct.

Masking

Often in watercolour, you want the white of the paper to represent the lightest areas of your subject. Sometimes you will need to protect the white areas so that they don't get splashed with paint accidentally. Masking is the way to do this. The masking technique can also be applied over a coloured wash. When a second wash is applied over the mask, the mask can then be removed to reveal the underlying base colour. This technique is used to give an aged and weathered look to paths, walls and painted timber.

There are many subjects that might benefit from masking, from whitewashed buildings and structural objects, such as ladders, to water foam splashing against a rock, tiny flowers, and even the delicate tracery of lace and spiders' webs.

There are three methods of applying masking. The one you choose will depend largely on whether you need to mask straight lines, delicate lines or curved shapes, or larger areas.

Masking tape

Masking tape is useful for masking straight-edged shapes, such as buildings, although it can also be cut or even torn to create more random effects. Make sure you use the low-tack variety of masking tape, otherwise you may find that you damage the surface of your watercolour paper when you attempt to remove it.

1 Place the masking tape on the watercolour paper, smoothing it down at the edges so that no paint can get underneath.

2 Apply a wash over the top of the masking tape and then leave it to dry completely.

3 Carefully peel off the tape (you may need to use the tip of a scalpel or craft or utility knife to lift the edge). The area underneath remains white.

Masking fluid

Masking fluid is useful when you want to mask out thin lines, such as grasses in the foreground of a landscape. You can also spatter it on to the paper for subjects such as white daisies in a meadow or the white foam of a waterfall.

Always wash the brush thoroughly with liquid detergent immediately after use, as it is almost impossible to remove the fluid from the bristles once it has dried; better still, keep old brushes specifically for use with masking fluid.

1 Using an old brush, paint masking fluid over the areas you want to protect. Leave it to dry completely.

2 Apply a wash over the paper and leave it to dry completely.

3 Using your fingertips, gently rub off the fluid. (You will find that it can be rubbed off quite easily.)

Masking film

Masking film (frisket paper) is used by draughtsmen and is available from most good art supply stores. It works best with large, clearly defined areas that you can easily cut around, such as hills or a pale-coloured building.

You need to use a very smooth watercolour paper or board so that the film has a perfectly flat surface to adhere to, otherwise paint may seep under the edges and ruin the effect.

Alternatively, you could cut a paper mask and either hold it in position with one hand while you paint with the other, or fix it to your painting surface with low-tack masking tape. This is not advisable for fiddly, intricate details where you need the mask to be stuck down firmly, but if you need to protect, say, the sky area of a landscape while you spatter paint on to the land, then a paper mask is a good, low-cost option.

1 Cut a piece of masking film (frisket paper) to roughly the same size as your painting. Peel the film from its backing paper, position it on your underdrawing, and smooth it down with a soft cloth or piece of tissue paper to make sure it is stuck down firmly and smoothly.

2 Using a scalpel or craft (utility) knife, carefully cut around the outer line of your subject, taking care not to cut into the paper or board.

3 Slowly peel back the masking film from the area that you do not want to protect from paint (ie. the area that you want to paint with colour).

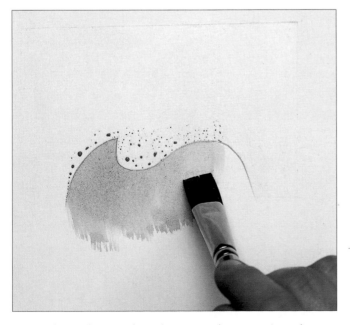

4 Apply a colour wash to the exposed paper, using a large round brush. Leave the wash to dry completely before you attempt to remove the masking film.

5 Check that the wash is dry, then slowly peel back the masking film from the unpainted area. Remove it in a smooth movement, so as not to tear the paper.

Practice exercise: **Masking a white-patterned jar**

This short exercise allows you to experiment with using both masking fluid (to mask out the sweeping curved lines and fine detail of the decorative jar) and low-tack masking tape (to mask out the straight-edged rectangle of paper on which the jar is placed). Painting around the pattern on the jar in order to leave the paper white would be a painstakingly slow and laborious process, and it would be very difficult to create such fine lines. Protecting the pattern with masking fluid allows you to work in a much more free and spontaneous manner.

Materials
- 2B pencil
- 200lb (425gsm) NOT watercolour paper, pre-stretched
- Watercolour paints: cobalt blue, ultramarine blue, Payne's grey, raw umber, dioxazine purple
- Brushes: old brush for masking, medium round, fine round
- Masking fluid
- Low-tack masking tape

The set-up
Arrange your subject on a piece of coloured paper that harmonizes with it, and position a table lamp in front of and slightly to the right of the subject so that you get an interesting shadow.

1 Using a 2B pencil, lightly sketch the jar and its decorative pattern. Using an old brush and liquid rubber masking fluid, mask out any areas that you want to keep white and clear of paint. Rinse the brush thoroughly and allow the masking fluid to dry completely before moving on to the next stage.

2 With the design protected by the masking fluid, there is no risk of accidentally painting over the white areas. Mix a vivid blue from cobalt blue, ultramarine blue and a little Payne's grey. Using a medium round brush, wash this mixture evenly over the jar. Leave to dry.

3 Using the same blue paint mixture, work over the jar once again to strengthen the tone. Add more Payne's grey to the mixture when you paint the right-hand side of the jar, which is slightly in shadow. This darker tone helps to make the jar look realistically three-dimensional. Leave to dry.

4 Using your fingertip, gently rub off the masking fluid. It should come off easily, but if any of the masking fluid is hard to remove, use a soft kneaded eraser. Blow or brush any bits of loose masking fluid off the paper before continuing.

5 Using the same blue mixture used in Step 2, carefully paint in the detailing on the pattern – the outline of the flowers, the flower centres, and tiny brushmarks to indicate the bark of the branches. Leave to dry. Mix a mid-toned Payne's grey and brush over those parts of the white patterns that are in shadow. This helps to integrate the stark design into the painting and reinforces the three-dimensional feel.

6 Using low-tack masking tape, mask out the square of dark grey paper on which the jar is standing. Mix a warm grey from Payne's grey and raw umber and, using a medium round brush, paint in the rectangular shape. Do not flood on too much paint, as there is always a risk that some may seep under the tape and ruin the clean edge. Leave to dry.

The finished painting

Once the tape has been removed, complete the painting by adding the dark shadow cast by the jar using a pale mauve mixed from Payne's grey and dioxazine purple. The result is an attractive little study that preserves the flowing lines and brilliant white pattern on the jar, without looking tight or laboured in its execution.

The brilliant white of the paper is preserved to the last.

The shadow anchors the jar on the surface.

Resists

Resist techniques are based on the principle that wax and water do not mix. Wax repels water, so if there is wax on your watercolour paper, any watercolour paint that is subsequently applied to those areas will not adhere to the surface.

Wax can be applied in several ways. You can use a clear wax candle, coloured wax crayons or oil pastels to draw on to the support. Interesting results can also be obtained by brushing on furniture wax using a stiff bristle brush. The technique is similar to using masking fluid but, unlike masking fluid, a resist cannot be removed.

Since the wax remains on the support and will continue to repel any subsequent washes, you need to plan where and at what point you introduce the resist. It does not have to be applied to the paper at the beginning of the work; you can introduce it at any point by working over existing dry washes.

The technique is difficult to use in confined, detailed areas and is more commonly used to create broader areas of texture. The success of the technique depends on how much pressure you apply and on the type of surface on which you are working. On a smooth, hot-pressed paper, the wax takes to the surface in a uniform way, resulting in a more subtle, flatter effect. On a rough paper, the wax is picked up only on the "peaks" of the paper surface, resulting in the wash lying in the "troughs", producing a highly textured, speckled effect.

An interesting variation can be made by combining it with frottage. Frottage allows you to incorporate textures other than that of the watercolour paper into your painting. Place smooth, lightweight paper on a textured surface, such as a plank of wood, and rub on the wax. The wax will pick up the texture of the underlying surface and, once a wash has been applied, the pattern will be revealed.

Resist techniques are ideal for light sea waves and for broken textural effects for sand and shingle. These patterns can be applied as a drawing or as a fragmented layer of light colour. Try drawing the white petals of a daisy with a wax resist and then covering them with deep blue – the contrasting tones are quite startling.

Household candle

Using an uncoloured household candle as a resist is an effective and inexpensive way of creating large areas of texture on a painting. Be aware that you cannot remove the wax once it has been applied, so don't get too carried away!

1 Rub a household candle over the paper, presssing quite hard to ensure that enough wax is deposited on the surface of the paper.

2 Apply a watercolour wash. Note how the wax repels the water in the paint. Here a rough paper was used, creating a broken texture.

On smooth, hot-pressed paper

On smooth, hot-pressed paper, the wax can be applied more smoothly. As a result, when the watercolour wash has been applied, the effect is much more subtle.

Coloured wax crayon or oil pastel

With a coloured wax crayon or oil pastel, not only can you make finer, more linear marks which will remain visible in the finished painting, but it is also easier to see exactly where the wax has been applied. This makes it less likely that you will apply too much of the resist that cannot then be removed, and it is a useful way to practise the resist technique.

1 Use the tip of the coloured wax crayon or oil pastel to draw in the areas where you want to apply the resist. Work slowly and in one smooth, continuous movement.

2 Apply a watercolour wash over the top of the resist The fine coloured lines of the wax remain visible, even though the wash was applied over the whole surface.

Practice exercise: **Using resists to create texture**

In this exercise, a combination of oil pastels and watercolour is used to give tiny variations in tone across the surface of the fruits, revealing the dimpled texture. Resists are used both to add colour and to reserve the white of the paper. The colour of the oil pastels is rich and vibrant, and it shows through the lighter watercolour washes because the oil in the pastels acts as a resist and repels the watercolour paint. Candle wax is used to reserve the white of the paper for the brightest highlights.

Materials
* *200lb (425gsm) NOT watercolour paper, pre-stretched*
* *2B pencil*
* *Watercolour paints: cadmium lemon, cadmium orange, burnt umber, sap green, Payne's grey, dioxazine purple*
* *Oil pastels: cadmium yellow, yellow ochre, deep orange*
* *Brushes: medium round*
* *Household candle*

The set-up
Odd numbers of objects always seem to work better in a still-life composition than even numbers. Arrange the fruit to form a composition that is roughly triangular in shape, with the lemon angled to "point" towards the oranges.

▶

1 Using a 2B pencil, lightly sketch the outline of the fruits, looking carefully at their positions in relation to one another and at where they overlap. Scribble in the lighter yellow areas using a cadmium yellow oil pastel. Take care not to press too heavily, or the pastel will build up in the tooth of the paper to such an extent that there will be nowhere for the watercolour wash to adhere to the paper.

2 Using a clear wax candle, draw the white highlight on each orange and on the lemon; the wax will repel the watercolour paint, with the result that these areas will remain white in the finished painting. Develop the colours on the oranges and lemon using yellow ochre and deep orange oil pastels. As before, keep the pastel marks light and open so that they help describe and follow the contours of the fruit.

3 Brush on the lightest washes – cadmium lemon on the lemon and cadmium orange on the oranges. The paint gathers and puddles on those areas of the paper that are free of oil pastel and candle wax. Leave to dry.

4 When dry, go back to the oil pastels to redraw areas and add colour and detail. Now that some paint has been applied, you can make this subsequent pastel work heavier, as it will not affect the washes that have been put down.

5 Using concentrated mixes of cadmium orange, cadmium lemon and burnt umber, paint the shaded sides of the fruits, and the areas where the stalks are attached, in order to make them look more rounded and three-dimensional. Allow the paint to puddle as before and leave to dry.

6 Mix a brownish green from sap green, cadmium orange and burnt umber and paint the point where the stalk is attached. Paint the shadow in Payne's grey and drop cadmium orange and dioxazine purple into the grey to hint at the colours reflected from the underside of the fruit.

The finished painting

This is a lively and spontaneous painting of a very simple still life. The oil pastel resists add both depth of colour and texture to the image, while the watercolour washes provide smoother, calmer areas that act as an effective contrast. Even the white highlight areas have gained some texture from the candlewax resist.

The bright highlighted areas of the fruits are reserved by using clear candle wax.

Yellow ochre and deep orange oil pastels convey the colours of the oranges and also repel the paint to create interesting textures.

Spattering

Spattering is an effective technique for creating texture in paintings. It consists of flicking paint on to the paper to create a random series of dots or flecks. It is done either by tapping a brush loaded with paint, so that drops of paint fall on the paper beneath, or by pulling back the bristles of a loaded brush with your fingers, so that paint droplets fly off.

You can apply spatter to either dry or wet paper, or even combine the two approaches in a single painting. They give very different effects. On a dry ground, the spatter doesn't blur, so this is a good technique for subjects such as old stone walls and pebbly garden paths, where you want the dots and flecks of paint to be crisp and sharp. On a wet surface, the spatter blurs and spreads, which can be useful for snow or foam-crested waves lapping against the shore.

The amount of water in the paint mixture affects the size of the spatter marks: the wetter the mixture, the larger the marks. Distance also plays a part: the further away you hold the brush, the smaller the marks and the wider the area that will be covered. Practise on scrap paper to find out how much pressure you need to apply and how far away from the paper you need to hold the brush in order to create the effect you want.

Pulling back the bristles
Load a stiff-bristled brush with paint and gently pull the bristles back towards you.

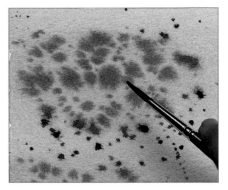

Tapping the brush
Load the brush with paint, hold it horizontally over the area that you want to spatter, and gently tap the handle.

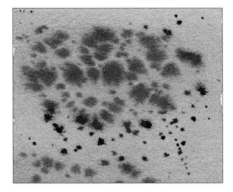

Spatter on a damp wash
Applied to a wet surface, the paint droplets blur and spread.

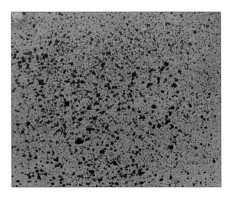

Spatter on a dry wash
Applied to a dry surface, the paint droplets remain crisp and well defined.

Practice exercise: **Beach with spattered pebbles**

Spattering is the perfect technique for this pebbly beach scene. Make the foreground spatters slightly larger than those in the distance. The foreground pebbles appear larger because they are closer to the viewer, so this will help to create an impression of distance.

Materials
- *2B pencil*
- *140lb (300gsm) rough watercolour paper, pre-stretched*
- *Watercolour paints: cobalt blue, raw sienna, light red, sepia, ultramarine violet, cadmium red, cadmium orange, Payne's grey*
- *Brushes: old brush for masking, large round, fine round*
- *Masking fluid*

The original scene
You can almost feel the hard, crunchy texture of this shingle beach. Spattering the paint on to dry paper will create crisp dots of texture.

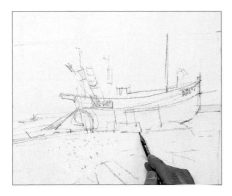

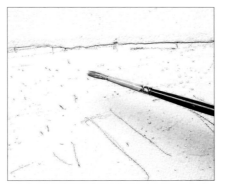

1 Using a 2B pencil, lightly sketch the outline of the boat and flags and the planks of wood that lie in the foreground of the beach scene.

2 Hold a piece of scrap paper over the boat to protect it and, using an old brush, spatter masking fluid over the beach. Leave to dry.

3 Dampen everything except the boat with water. Brush pale cobalt blue over the sky. Brush a mixture of raw sienna and light red over the beach.

4 When the previous stage is dry, mix a dark brown from sepia, ultramarine violet and a little light red and paint the boat, adding more ultramarine violet for the stern. Use a pale version of the mixture for the planks and brush broad strokes of the same colour across the beach. Paint the flags in cobalt blue and the floats in a mixture of cadmium red and cadmium orange. Using a fine brush, paint around the lettering in Payne's grey.

5 Mix a warm brown from raw sienna and sepia. Hold a piece of scrap paper over the boat to protect it and, using a fine brush, spatter the paint mixture over the foreground.

6 Add ultramarine violet to the mixture to darken it and continue spattering as before. Using the same mixture, darken the ropes tethering the boat and the planks. Leave to dry.

The finished painting
Complete the picture by rubbing off the masking fluid. This is a delightful little scene of a beach at low tide. The spattering is subtle and does not detract from the painting of the boat, but it captures the texture of the hard, shingly beach very effectively.

These stripes of colour help to imply the ripples in the sand.

The spattering in the foreground contrasts well with the flat colour of the sky.

Stippling

Stippling consists of placing dots or blobs of colour on the paper. The techique is often used to create texture in a painting, but it can also be used to optically mix colours on the paper, as it was by the French Pointillist School, whose most famous exponent was Georges Seurat (1859–91).

The dots can be placed close together or further apart, depending on the effect you want to create. You can use either a specialist stippling brush, which is a short, stubby brush with hard bristles, or the tip of your normal painting brush. To create even stipples, dip an almost dry brush into a thick mix of watercolour paint. A wetter mix of paint will produce dots that are less sharply defined.

The technique
Load a stippling brush with paint and, holding the brush almost vertically, dab it on to the paper with short, sharp movements. Vary the amount of pressure to create dots of different weights.

The effect
A stippling brush creates areas of random texture that are perfect for subjects such as lichen-covered pebbles and stones.

Practice exercise: **Fruits with stippled texture**

Stippling is a great way of painting fruits with dimpled surfaces, such as the citrus fruits and avocado shown here. Use a fine brush and stipple darker tones on to the base colours of the fruits to convey the pitted hollows in the skin.

The set-up
When you set up a still-life exercise like this, position a table or anglepoise lamp to one side. The raking light will pick out the dimples on the fruit, making it easier for you to see where to apply the stippling, and will cast interesting shadows that make the subject look three-dimensional.

Materials
- *2B pencil*
- *140lb (300gsm) rough watercolour paper, pre-stretched*
- *Watercolour paints: aureolin, yellow ochre, raw sienna, sap green, Payne's grey, ultramarine blue, burnt umber, ultramarine violet*
- *Brushes: fine-pointed old brush for masking, medium round, fine round*
- *Masking fluid*

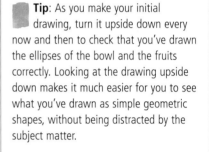

Tip: As you make your initial drawing, turn it upside down every now and then to check that you've drawn the ellipses of the bowl and the fruits correctly. Looking at the drawing upside down makes it much easier for you to see what you've drawn as simple geometric shapes, without being distracted by the subject matter.

1 Using a 2B pencil, lightly sketch the outline of your subject. Using an old, fine brush, stipple masking fluid on any highlight areas on the left-hand side, where light hits the fruit. Leave to dry completely.

2 Mix two washes, one from aureolin with a little yellow ochre and the other from yellow ochre alone. Dampen the foreground lemon and bowl with clean water. Paint the lemon with the aureolin and yellow ochre mixture and the bowl in the plain yellow ochre.

3 Mix raw sienna with a little yellow ochre and, while the paper is still damp, touch this mixture on to the right-hand side of the bowl, which is in shadow. Add a little sap green to the mixture and brush it on to the shadowed side of the foreground lemon. Paint the lemon in the bowl with the aureolin and yellow ochre mixture used in Step 2. Leave to dry.

4 Mix a pale green colour from sap green and aureolin. Wet the limes and the avocado with clean water. While the paper is still damp, using a medium round brush, brush this mixture over the limes, leaving some white areas untouched where the light hits the fruits. Add some Payne's grey to the mixture and stipple it over the avocado. Leave to dry.

5 Mix a dark green from ultramarine blue and sap green. Using a fine round brush, stipple the mixture over the darker areas of the limes and leave to dry. Mix sap green with a little Payne's grey and wash this mixture over the right-hand side of the avocado and the shadowed underside of the lime in the bowl. Leave to dry.

6 Strengthen the tone on the bowl by applying another wash of yellow ochre, leaving a white edge on the rim. Add a touch of burnt umber to the inside of the bowl. Leave to dry. Stipple a mixture of aureolin and yellow ochre on to the foreground lemon, adding burnt umber for the side that is in shadow. Stipple a mixture of sap green and Payne's grey on to the dark side of the avocado and the foreground lime. Leave to dry.

The finished painting

To complete the painting, rub off the masking fluid to reveal the brightest highlights. Next, paint the shadows by dropping a very pale wash of ultramarine violet and burnt umber wet into wet on to dampened paper. Random stippling conveys the texture of the fruits and contrasts well with the wet-into-wet washes used on the smooth china bowl.

The brightest highlights are left unpainted, protected by masking fluid until the final stages.

Random stippling conveys the pitted surface of the fruits perfectly.

The shadows help to anchor the painting and show that the subject is not floating in mid-air.

Drybrush

In the drybrush technique, paint is put on with a brush that is quickly skimmed over the paper, leaving the colour on the ridges of the surface but not in the troughs. As you might expect, the brush should be fairly dry. If either the paper or the brush is too wet, the indentations of the paper will quickly fill with colour. Keep a piece of kitchen paper close to hand so that you can dab off any paint that is too wet.

The drybrush technique is useful for subjects such as wood bark or ageing stonework, and for foreground grasses. Because drybrush work is often used in the final stages of a painting, to add texture and visual interest, it is a good idea to test your loaded brush on a piece of scrap paper before you use the technique in your almost completed work.

Using a round brush
Dip the brush in your chosen paint colour and, using your fingertips, squeeze out any excess paint so that the brush is almost dry and splay out the bristles. Drag the brush over the surface of the paper. It will make broken, textured marks.

Using a fan brush
A fan brush, in which the bristles are naturally splayed, allows you to cover a wider area of the paper.

Practice exercise: **Lily with drybrushed leaves and buds**

The drybrush technique is perfect for subjects with slightly broken textures, such as leaf forms. On rough paper, dragging an almost dry brush across these areas will give an immediacy and freshness to the painting.

Materials
- 2B pencil
- 140lb (300gsm) rough watercolour paper, pre-stretched
- Watercolour paints: aureolin, sap green, yellow ochre, rose madder deep, ultramarine blue, cadmium orange
- Brushes: medium round, fine round
- Kneaded eraser
- Kitchen paper

Tip: If you find it hard to get the shape of the half-open lily flower right, try to think of it as a simple geometric shape – such as an inverted cone – on top of which you superimpose an ellipse and the triangular shapes of the individual petals. Taking an objective approach to your subject can be helpful when dealing with irregular shapes.

The set-up
Position your subject on a large sheet of white paper: this is a good way of practising the technique, without having to worry about painting a complicated background. Turn the lily around until you find an angle that allows you to see the inside of the half-opened flower.

1 Using a 2B pencil, make a light sketch of the lily. It is important to count the number of petals and leaves beforehand, and to work out the position of each one carefully.

2 Mix a yellowish green from aureolin, sap green and a little yellow ochre. Holding an almost dry brush vertically, paint the buds. Add more sap green and paint the leaves in the same way.

3 Continue putting in the leaves in the same way. Use a slightly darker version of the same mixture for the stalks and one edge of some of the main leaves, so that the painting starts to take on a three-dimensional quality.

4 Mix a dark pink colour from rose madder deep and drybrush it on to the petals of the open lily flower.

5 Mix a very pale ultramarine blue and paint the shadow on the underside of the petals. Paint the stamens in cadmium orange. Using a fine round brush, stipple tiny dots of the dark pink colour inside the petals.

6 Mix a dark green from ultramarine blue and sap green and, using a fine round brush, drybrush this mixture over the leaves to paint the veins. Paint the same colour on the unopened buds to delineate the individual petals.

The finished painting

Rub out some of the superfluous pencil markings with a kneaded eraser and the painting is complete. Working on dry paper, with an almost dry brush, is the perfect way to delineate the fine leaf forms and the lines that separate the petals of this lily. The technique has also allowed the texture of the paper to show through, creating a painting that is full of visual interest.

The drybrush work on the leaves has created an interesting texture.

Warm and cool colours help to make the lily look three-dimensional: the warm rose advances, while the cooler purple recedes.

Sponging

Sponges can be used to lift off unwanted colour while the paper is still damp (for example, to wipe out clouds in a dark sky) and instead of a brush to dampen paper. However, the main purpose of sponging is to produce texture.

Natural sponges are more randomly textured than synthetic ones, which have a very regular pattern. Experiment with different kinds to find out what kind of marks they make. You can sponge on to dry or damp paper. On damp paper, the marks will merge together, while on dry paper they will be more crisply defined.

Sponging is a useful technique for painting stone walls and pebbled paths and beaches. It is also excellent for misty trees and anything that needs a soft edging, and for creating the effect of lichen on walls and wooden gates.

The technique
Wet the sponge so that it is soft and pliable and squeeze out any excess water. Dip the sponge in your chosen paint (you will need to mix a large wash, as the sponge is very absorbent). Gently dab it on to the paper.

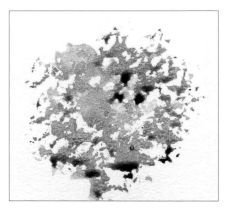

The effect
The sponge leaves a series of pitted marks that are ideal for conveying texture. This technique is particularly useful for painting clumps of foliage.

Practice exercise: **Removing and adding colour with a sponge**

In this exercise, sponging is used both to remove paint, softening colours applied with a brush, and to add it, creating small areas of soft texture.

Materials
- *300lb (640gsm) rough watercolour paper*
- *Watercolour paints: alizarin crimson, Prussian blue, cadmium lemon, ultramarine blue, cadmium yellow*
- *Brushes: medium round*
- *Small sponge*

The original scene
This array of bouquets on a market stall is almost overpoweringly colourful. The artist decided to paint a single bouquet in order to concentrate on the effects created from the sponging technique.

1 Mix a deep pink from alizarin crimson with a tiny amount of Prussian blue. Using a medium round brush, loosely paint the shapes of the outer ring of flowers in the bouquet.

2 While this paint is still wet, dampen a small sponge in clean water and squeeze out any excess moisture. Wipe the sponge over the paint around the inner edge of the ring of flowers, removing colour and softening the brush marks. This creates the basis for a ring of lighter-coloured flowers.

3 Dilute the pink mixture used in Step 1 by adding more water. Dip the sponge into the mixture and gently dab it into the empty centre of the bouquet to reduce the starkness of the white.

4 You may find that the centre now looks too dark. If so, rinse the sponge in clear water and squeeze out any excess moisture. Gently wipe the sponge over the centre of the bouquet to remove some of the colour you have just applied and soften any hard edges.

5 Load the sponge with a more highly pigmented version of the mixture used in Step 3 and gently dab it into the centre of the bouquet, to create an inner ring of flowers, and around the outer ring to create some texture and more depth of colour in this area.

6 Using a slightly bluer version of the mixture and a medium round brush, loosely delineate the edges of individual flowers within the bouquet and around the outer rim.

The finished painting

Complete the painting by lightly brushing in the foliage around the outside of the bouquet, using a light green mixed from cadmium lemon and a little ultramarine blue and a darker green mixed from cadmium yellow and ultramarine blue and paint the darkest outer leaves in the same way. This is a loose, but lively, interpretation which owes much of its success to the random sponging technique, used here both to add colour and to remove it.

Light, calligraphic brushstrokes for the leaves complement the loose textures created with the sponge.

Sponging on the outer ring of flowers has created tonal variety and a sense of depth.

Additives

There are all kinds of materials that can be added to the brush or mixed into watercolour paint. Some materials alter the characteristics of the paint, while others create textures that could not be achieved using a brush alone. These additives should be used in moderation and only in carefully selected areas of the painting, as they can easily become too dominant and detract from the effect of the work as a whole, but they are useful additional tools in your armoury.

Additives that alter the characteristics of the paint

One of the most useful additives in this category is gum arabic. Adding a few drops to your paint mixture has two effects. First, it slows down the drying time, giving you more time to work. Second, it gives the paint a slight sheen, which is particularly useful when you are painting shiny or varnished surfaces such as a wooden table in a still life. Gum arabic also makes colours appear stronger and more saturated. Glycerin will also slow down the drying time and makes the paint slightly sticky and easier to control on the paper.

Another additive that changes the characteristics of the paint is granulation medium. Some colours, such as French ultramarine, granulate naturally, but this medium allows you to exploit that characteristic with any colour, although it works better with darker colours and ones that have a natural tendency to granulate.

Gum arabic
Pour a few drops of gum arabic into pre-mixed watercolour paint and mix thoroughly. Apply the paint to the paper with a brush. Because the gum arabic retards the paint's drying time, you can then work into it with a palette knife or the tip of a brush handle.

Granulation medium
Add a few drops of granulation medium to pre-mixed watercolour paint and mix thoroughly. Apply the paint to the paper as normal. When the paint dries, it will have a slightly speckled, granular appearance. This is an effective way of painting old, worn stonework.

Additives for texture

Texture pastes and gels can be applied directly to the paper with a palette knife or mixed with watercolour paint first and brushed on. When they dry, the surface is slightly raised. Paint applied on top of the raised surface will settle in intriguing ways.

Sand, grit, tissue paper and other textured materials can be added to glue. Apply the glue to your painting, stir or press the required material into the glue, and allow to dry thoroughly before painting on top.

Finally, common household salt can create some exciting effects. Drop salt into a wet watercolour wash and leave to dry before brushing off the crystals. The salt leaches the colour out of the watercolour. The result depends on how wet the wash is: if it is too wet, the effect will not be so pronounced, and if it is too dry the salt will have no effect.

Texture medium
This is a viscous, white-coloured fluid. Mix it thoroughly into the pre-mixed watercolour paint, or apply it directly to the paper, and stipple it on to the painting surface with a palette knife. When the paint dries, the surface will be slightly raised.

Salt
Sprinkle common household salt on to a wet wash. When it is completely dry, gently brush off the salt crystals. The salt will leach the colour out of the paint, leaving mottled marks. This is a useful technique for painting snow or textured subjects, such as lichen.

Practice exercise: **Textured stone and iron**

In this study of a rusty chain on a worn, lichen-encrusted harbour wall, the artist has indulged in a little lateral thinking: if salt can create interesting textures, why not see what you can achieve with other items from the kitchen? Here, olive oil and plain white flour have been used as inexpensive alternatives to oil-pastel or candlewax resists and texture medium. Don't feel constrained by convention: painting should be all about experimenting and having fun.

Materials
- HB pencil
- 220lb (450gsm) rough watercolour paper, unstretched
- Watercolour paints: yellow ochre, burnt umber, cadmium red, alizarin crimson, ultramarine blue, Naples yellow, burnt sienna
- Gouache paints: Chinese white
- Brushes: medium flat, medium round, fine round, large wash
- Olive oil
- Salt: fine-grained, coarse-grained
- Flour

The original scene
The lovely, subtle colours on this old stone wall give you the opportunity to work wet into wet, allowing the colours to merge on the paper. The speckled textures in the wall provide additional visual interest, while the chain forms a diagonal line across the frame, giving a dynamic composition.

1 Using an HB pencil, sketch the subject, indicating the position of the chain and rope and the main bands of colour on the wall behind. Look at how the links of the chain are joined and at how the rope loops twist and fall over each other: the composition is very simple, but elements such as this are key to making it look realistic.

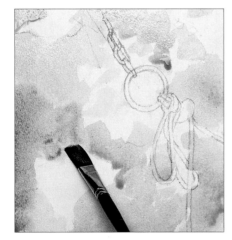

2 Mix three very pale washes for the background colours: yellow ochre, burnt umber, and a pinkish mixture of yellow ochre, cadmium red and alizarin crimson. Using a medium flat brush, dab yellow ochre on at the top of the paper, burnt umber at the base, and the pink mixture on the left-hand side. Dampen any unpainted areas with clean water so that the whole paper is wet.

3 While the first washes are still wet, dip a medium round brush in olive oil and dab large and small marks into the washes. The oil acts as a resist and repels watercolour paint, and will give a mottled appearance when dry – although, because the oil is applied on top of the watercolour, rather than the other way round, the effect is subtle and understated.

4 Mix a dark brown from burnt umber and ultramarine blue and dab it on to the darker areas at the base of the picture. While it is still wet, dab on more olive oil. Leave to dry. Mix a pale, rusty brown colour from burnt umber, alizarin crimson, Naples yellow and ultramarine blue. Using a fine round brush, paint the iron chain and ring.

▶

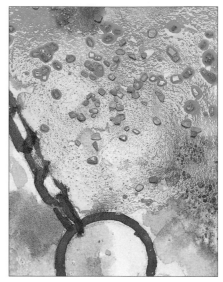

5 Add a little ultramarine blue to the pinkish mixture used in Step 2 to make an orangey brown. Using a large wash brush, dab the mixture over the left-hand side of the wall. While this is still wet, sprinkle a little fine-grained salt over it.

6 Mix an opaque, creamy yellow from yellow ochre and Chinese white gouache. Using a medium round brush, dot it on to the chain and the salted area on the left of the picture. This area is still damp, so the paint spreads a little and looks like small patches of lichen.

7 Add burnt sienna and ultramarine blue to the opaque yellow mixture used in Step 6 to make a pale, bluish grey. Using a medium round brush, dab the mixture over the light area at the top of the wall. Sprinkle on some coarse-grained salt.

8 Mix an opaque pinkish grey from yellow ochre, alizarin crimson, Naples yellow, a little ultramarine blue and Chinese white gouache. Brush it over the shaded parts of the chain and ring; suddenly they look three-dimensional. Add more ultramarine blue to the mixture and paint inside the rope loops and around the chain. Mix a dark brown from burnt umber, ultramarine blue and a little alizarin crimson and paint inside the ring.

9 Using a medium round brush, dab the same dark brown mixture on to the left-hand side of the wall. Sprinkle flour into the wet areas; it will sink into the wet paint in clumps, leaving a slightly raised surface when it dries.

10 Outline the links of the chain in pure burnt sienna, taking care to break the line where the links overlap to give a three-dimensional effect.

Tip: Take plenty of time over this stage and study your reference photo carefully: these dark lines indicate how the links of the chain are joined together, so it's important to get them right.

11 Mix a pale blue from ultramarine blue, burnt sienna and Chinese white gouache. Paint the rope strands and the shadows underneath the rope.

12 Mix Chinese white gouache with a tiny amount of ultramarine blue and paint the mortar lines in the brickwork of the wall.

13 Gently brush off the dry salt crystals to reveal mottled, bleached-out marks that look like lichen growing on the harbour wall.

The finished painting

Often, insignificant details can make intriguing paintings: there is nothing exceptional about this subject, but the soft colours and contrasts of texture make it very appealing. The artist has applied a number of additives – some more unusual and unorthodox than others – to the wet watercolour washes, thereby creating interesting textures that could not have been achieved by brushwork alone.

Salt leaches colour out of the paint, creating a mottled effect like lichen.

The flour has dried on to the paint in lumps, creating a slightly raised surface that looks like worn, uneven stonework.

Line and wash

Combining inks with watercolours – a technique that is commonly known as line and wash – is one of the most challenging and exciting of all watercolour techniques. It enables you to combine the precise detail of pen-and-ink work with the fluidity and transparency of watercolour washes.

It doesn't matter whether you do the ink drawing or the watercolour washes first; that really depends on what you want to say about your subject. The real danger, especially for beginners, is putting in too much linear detail and consequently overworking the picture. Make a conscious effort to simplify your subject and put down only the essentials.

The key to a successful line-and-wash painting is to maintain a balance between the two media. Although there are no hard-and-fast rules, a useful guideline is that if your subject contains relatively little colour you can afford to do a lot of pen work, while a very colourful subject will probably require less. (Lots of pen work in a painting of a colourful flower border, for example, would detract from the colours of the subject; with an action subject such as a dancer or sporting scene, you might choose to make the pen work tell most of the story, applying just a little colour for atmosphere.) It takes a certain amount of practice and skill to get the balance right.

Experiment with different inks, as there are both waterproof and water-soluble kinds. If you want the pen marks to be permanent, use waterproof inks. Water-soluble ink marks will blur and run when you apply watercolour washes on top of them, but you can create some exciting effects in this way.

Try different kinds of pen, too, to find out which ones you like using, and use the back of the nib, as well as the tip, to create different widths of line. Steel-nibbed dip pens make lovely lines, but they hold relatively little ink and you may find it frustrating to have to keep stopping to re-load the pen. Fountain pens and technical drawing pens have an ink reservoir, but the quality of line that they make may be a little too neat and regular for some people's tastes.

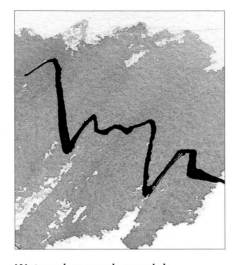

Watercolour wash over ink
Provided you use waterproof ink, as here, and allow it to dry completely, the lines will remain permanent and unsmudged even when you apply a watercolour wash over the top.

Semi-opaque paint over ink
The top half of the image shows a mixture of watercolour paint and permanent gouache applied over ink: the semi-opaque paint partially covers the ink, making the lines more muted. Compare this with the deep lines of the ink covered by pure watercolour in the bottom half of the image.

Practice exercise: **Church spire in line and wash**

Line and wash is the perfect technique for architectural subjects such as this picturesque church steeple and spire. Details can be held sharply in ink while watercolour washes provide colour and tonal variety. The dip pen used here provides a less regular and mechanical quality of line than a technical drawing pen, which helps to make the study of the building more lively.

Materials
- *2B pencil*
- *300lb (640gsm) rough watercolour paper*
- *Watercolour paints: yellow ochre, raw umber, ultramarine blue, cadmium red, burnt sienna, ultramarine blue, cadmium yellow*
- *Brushes: medium round*
- *Medium-nibbed steel dip pen*
- *Black waterproof ink*

The original scene
There is a lot of interesting detail in this scene. The arched bell-tower windows and a rounded turret cry out to be depicted in a crisp, linear way, while the soft transitions from light to dark tones in the stonework require soft-edged wet-into-wet washes.

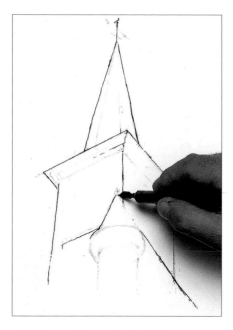

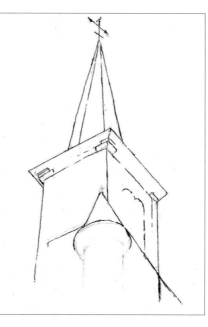

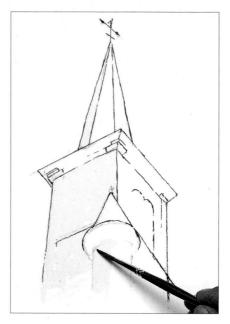

1 Using a 2B pencil, sketch the building. (If you are confident, start working in pen and ink straight away – but you cannot erase mistakes.) Using a medium dip pen and waterproof black ink, ink over the pencil lines.

2 Continue with the pen-and-ink work until you have put in all the main lines of the spire, steeple and rounded turret. Leave to dry completely before going on to the next stage of the painting.

3 Mix a pale wash of yellow ochre. Using a medium round brush put in the lightest tone, which is on the left-hand side of the steeple and spire. This establishes the underlying colour of the honey-coloured stonework.

4 Mix a mid-toned grey from raw umber with a little ultramarine blue. Put in the second facet of the spire, the shadow under the eave on the left, and the roof of the rounded turret. Add a little cadmium red and paint the right-hand side of the steeple, painting around the arched window.

5 Mix a dark brown from burnt sienna and ultramarine blue and put in the darkest facet of the steeple, the side that is in shade. The building is now starting to look three-dimensional, and this will be reinforced in the later stages of the painting.

▶

6 Mix a rich, orangey-brown from cadmium yellow, cadmium red and a little ultramarine blue and paint the rounded turret. Use the dark brown mixture from Step 5 to paint the shaded right-hand side of the turret and the eaves under the right-hand side of both the steeple and turret.

7 Using the orangey-brown mixture from Step 6, "draw" concentric lines underneath the conical roof of the turret so that you begin to establish the form of this structure. Paint the window in the turret in the same colour. Darken the mixture and paint under the eave on the right-hand side of the steeple.

8 Darken the middle facet of the spire using the dark brown mixture from Step 5. Using the steel-nibbed dip pen and waterproof black ink, reinforce some of the structural lines of the building and put in the curves of the arched window on the left-hand side of the steeple.

9 The right-hand side of the steeple looks too light, so mix a warm brown from ultramarine blue and cadmium red and darken it. Mix a neutral mauve from yellow ochre and ultramarine blue and paint the window on the right-hand side of the steeple.

10 Brush pale yellow ochre over the left-hand side to warm up the colour of the stone. Use the dark brown mixture from Step 5 to paint the recessed window on the left. Paint horizontal and vertical lines to the left of and below the window, indicating that the façade is not completely flush.

The finished painting

The artist has achieved a good balance between linear pen work and watercolour washes, with the ink establishing the structure and some of the fine detail of the building and the watercolour the subtle tonal transitions from light to dark.

On its own the pen work could have looked rather tight and mechanical, but successive layers of watercolour washes have helped to enliven the study and provide it with some depth and colour.

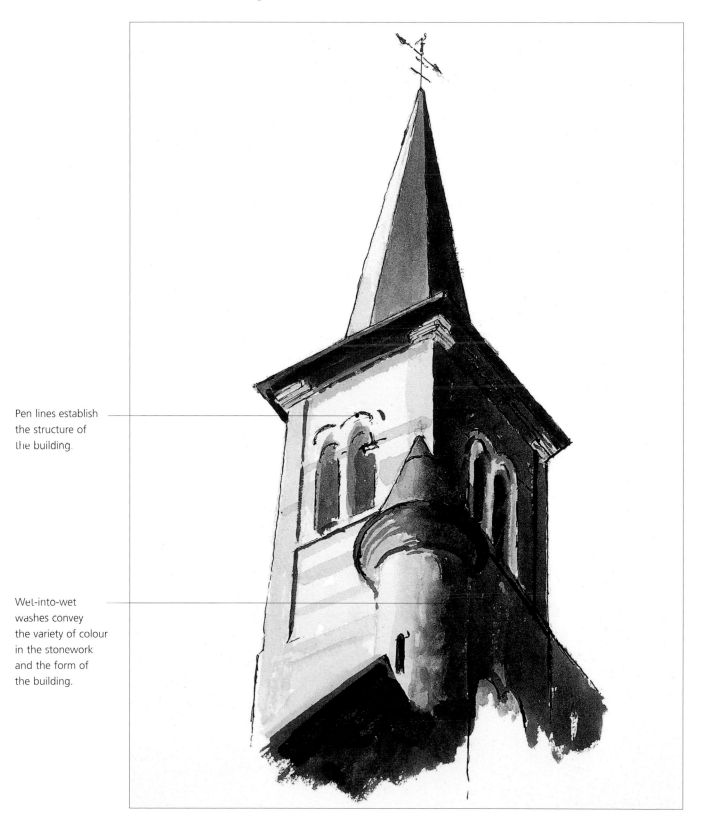

Pen lines establish the structure of the building.

Wet-into-wet washes convey the variety of colour in the stonework and the form of the building.

Water-soluble pencils

The advantage of water-soluble pencils is that they combine the linear appeal of pencil work with the fluidity of transparent watercolour washes. They are incredibly versatile: you can use them wet or dry, on their own or in conjunction with other media, and the colours do not go muddy. Easily portable, water-soluble pencils are a real boon when it comes to making sketches on location, but they are equally useful in the studio.

Water-soluble pencils are available in a breathtaking range of colours – there are far more shades available than you will find in any range of paints. You can also blend several colours together on the paper to produce subtler shades. However, some brands of water-soluble pencil seem to blend better than others, so it is worth experimenting with different brands in order to find one that you like.

Dry on dry
Applied dry on top of dry paper or watercolour washes, water-soluble pencils can be used to draw fine lines and details, such as veins in flower petals and leaves, feathers, mortar lines in brickwork, wood-grain effects, and highlighting on objects such as bottles.

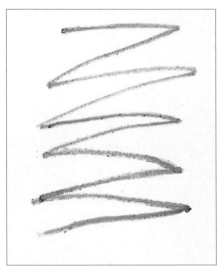

Wet on dry
Dipping the tip of the pencil in water before you apply it to the dry paper has two effects: it intensifies the colour and it also fixes the pencil marks, so that they do not blur (or do not blur as much) when a watercolour wash is applied on top.

Dry marks brushed with water
If water or a watercolour wash is brushed over dry water-soluble pencil marks, they will blur and spread a little – a useful technique for implying that objects are far away, such as a distant woodland. (Foreground details should always be crisp and sharp.)

Blending water-soluble pencil marks
Brushing clean water over water-soluble pencil marks will allow you to blend colours together easily.

> **Tip**: Make heavy scribbles in a range of colours and use them as easily portable "palettes": when you brush the scribbles with clean water, you can pick up enough colour on the brush to work with them in the same way as watercolour paints. However, the "paints" thus produced are generally less intense in colour than real watercolour paints.

Practice exercise: **Peacock feathers**

This exercise demonstrates the linear characteristics of using water-soluble pencils dry, and it gives you the chance to practise mixing colours optically by overlaying one colour on top of another. It also shows how the colour intensifies into a smooth, velvety finish when the tips of the pencils are dipped in water and used wet. For the best effect, use a smooth, HP paper.

Materials
- *HP paper, unstretched*
- *Water-soluble pencils: yellow-green, jade green, orange, light violet, light green, dark green, emerald green, turquoise, light blue, ultramarine blue, ivory black*

The display
When a male peacock displays, his tail feathers fan out into a shimmering mass of iridescent colours. Although you won't find true iridescent colours in your range of water-soluble pencils, you can come close to recreating the effect by carefully overlaying colours on the paper, so that they mix optically.

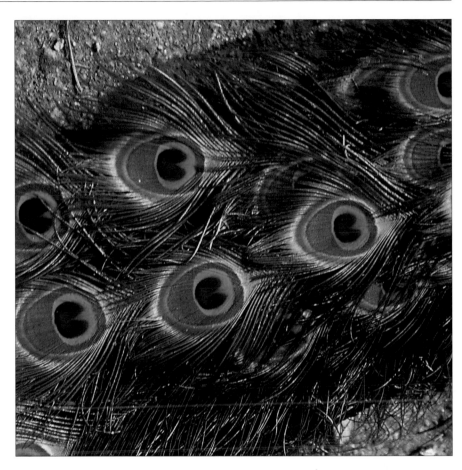

1 Outline the "eyes" of the peacock feathers with a pale, yellow-green line. Draw around the outside of the yellow lines with a jade green pencil.

2 Using the jade green pencil again, draw long, feathery strokes on the outer edges of the eyes. Draw an orange line inside the first yellow-green lines and fill in the lower half of the eyes in orange.

▶

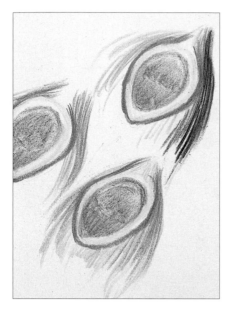

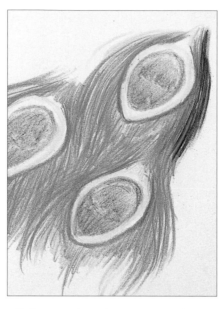

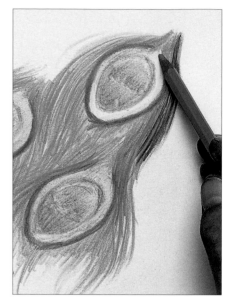

3 Fill in the upper half of the eyes with light violet. Following the direction of the peacock feathers, draw light green marks over the straggly jade green feathers, so that the two greens blend optically. Then repeat the process using a dark green pencil.

4 Go over the other greens again, and the large spaces between the eyes, with an emerald green pencil – again, making sure that your pencil marks follow the direction in which the feathers grow. Take care not to block in the colour too heavily.

5 Draw around the outside of the eyes with a turquoise pencil and draw over the initial yellow-green lines with jade green. Note how you are beginning to build up the depth of colour while still maintaining the linear quality of the pencil work.

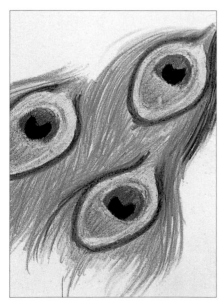

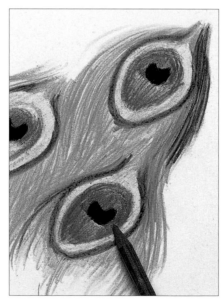

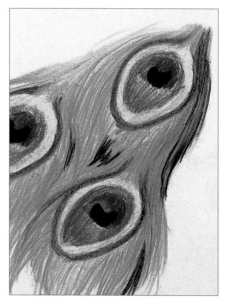

6 Go over the light violet of the eyes with a light blue pencil. Although you can't really see the underlying violet any more, the colours merge on the paper to create a purplish blue that you could not have created by using just one pencil on its own. Draw the "pupils" of the eyes in ivory black. (Note the irregular shape: they are not a neat circle or semi-circle.)

7 Dip the tip of an orange pencil in water and go over the orange colour again. Note how using the pencil wet intensifies the colour and creates a smooth, velvety block of colour in which the individual pencil strokes can no longer be clearly differentiated.

8 Strengthen the green feathers further by applying layers of emerald green and light green pencil. As before, follow the direction of the feathers and take care not to block in the colours completely, otherwise the feathers will look like a solid mass rather than individual strands. Draw in small touches of ivory black between the feathers: this adds drama.

9 The green markings look a little too green at this stage; you need to relieve the intensity and also hint at the iridescence of the feathers. Go over the green markings in places with an ultramarine blue pencil. Dip the ultramarine blue pencil in water and intensify the blue of the eye. Strengthen the orange of the eye in the same way.

10 Dip a dark green pencil in water and go over any areas that you want to be very dark. Because the pencil is used wet, the resulting marks are very smooth and intense in colour. Dip an ivory black pencil in water and build up more of the base feathers. This provides a background against which the colours will stand out more strongly.

The finished work

More a drawing than a painting, this little detail sketch nonetheless shows the range of marks and intensity of colour that can be produced with water-soluble pencils. It is also a lovely example of optical colour mixing.

Greens and blues intermingle to create subtle optical mixes that hint at the iridescence of the feathers.

The individual pencil strokes can clearly be seen.

More solid blocks of colour are achieved by dipping the tip of the pencil in water.

Using a toned ground

Although it is more usual for traditional transparent watercolour to be painted on white paper, it is possible – and, in some cases, even preferable – to work on a coloured or toned ground or paper.

Using a toned ground can create a colour harmony as, to a greater or lesser extent, the colour of the ground influences the colour of the washes that are applied over the top. It establishes a colour key that can help create a mood. A toned ground can also simplify and cut down considerably on the amount of time it takes to paint the picture: applying a wash over the whole paper in order to establish a colour key is often the first stage in making a watercolour painting.

Ready-prepared watercolour papers are available from art stores in shades of cream, oatmeal, grey, light blue and light green. If you require another colour, you will need to prepare the paper yourself by applying a wash of the desired hue in either watercolour or acrylic paint. Acrylic paint has the additional advantage of being permanent: there is no risk of the colour being disturbed by subsequent layers of watercolour washes. However, it does leave a slight residue and seals the surface, and this can affect the way the watercolour lies on the paper.

The toned ground need not be flat and uniform. If appropriate to the subject, you could create a textured ground using sponges or rough brush work.

The colour you choose for the ground should reflect the mood and atmosphere of the piece and complement the colours to be used. This is particularly important when using transparent watercolour. If you are using opaque watercolour (that is, watercolour to which body colour has been added), the opacity and covering power of the paint make the colour of the ground less noticeable.

If you are using opaque watercolour, the colour of the toned ground can lean towards the complementary colour of the main colours in the painting – for example, a predominantly green landscape on a pale red ground. Because of the effect of simultaneous contrast, a ground in a contrasting colour can make the colours used in the painting seem brighter.

Practice exercise: **Log and axe on toned ground**

This exercise shows how to create an overall colour harmony by using a toned ground. When you first start experimenting with toned grounds, keep the subject very simple, with a limited colour range, and think carefully about what colour will work best. Here, the overall colour of the wooden log and axe is a warm brown and so a pale, warm ground is the obvious choice.

Materials
- *2B pencil*
- *Soft graphite pencil*
- *200lb (425gsm) NOT watercolour paper, pre-stretched*
- *Watercolour paints: yellow ochre, burnt umber, Payne's grey, raw umber, ivory black, burnt sienna*
- *Brushes: large wash, medium round*

The set-up
The plain cream paper on which the log is set is helpful in some ways, because it allows you to see the cast shadow very clearly, but it is also very stark and bright and detracts from the subject.

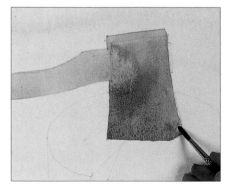

1 Tone the paper with a pale wash of yellow ochre. Leave to dry. Using a 2B pencil, sketch the outline of the axe and log. Paint the axe handle in a dilute wash of raw umber. Mix a light brown from burnt umber and Payne's grey and paint the axe head. Leave to dry.

2 Mix a dark brown from burnt umber and ivory black and paint the dark on the side and bottom of the axe head. Add raw umber and burnt sienna to the mixture and paint the handle, leaving the underlying colour where the light hits the handle. Leave to dry.

3 Add a little Payne's grey and plenty of water to the mixture to lighten the colour, then paint the side and top of the log. Using a slightly darker version of the same mixture, begin to paint some of the growth rings on the top of the log, but leave the split in the wood unpainted as parts of it are considerably lighter in tone than the surrounding wood.

4 Paint a series of fine burnt umber lines along the length of the axe handle to suggest the grain and pattern in the polished wood. Mix a warm brown from burnt umber and raw umber and paint the side of the log, using the side of the brush and a slight scrubbing action in order to create a broken, uneven texture.

5 Using the same raw umber and burnt umber mixture, paint the growth rings on the top of the log. Add burnt umber and Payne's grey to the mixture and paint the shadow inside the split. Using a soft graphite pencil, indicate the grain and growth rings on the side and top of the log. Once dry, rework the dark shadows deep within the split.

The finished painting

Crisp shadows painted in a warm grey mixed from Payne's grey and a little burnt umber complete the image and make it look three-dimensional. The yellow ochre ground harmonizes well with the colours used to paint the axe and log, whereas a white ground would have looked too stark and would have competed for the viewer's attention. It makes a subtle but important contribution to the overall warm tone of the image.

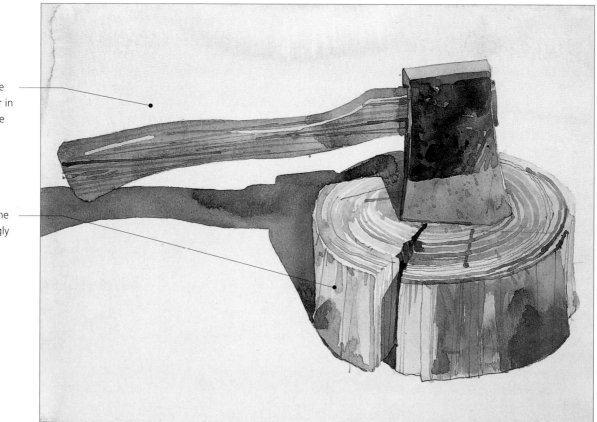

The yellow ochre ground is similar in colour to the axe and log.

The texture of the log is convincingly portrayed.

Working into wet paint

Watercolour washes can be manipulated in several ways when they are wet. They can be moved around, removed or worked into using various tools. The only restriction is the amount of time available before the paint dries to such an extent that it is no longer movable.

Certain papers facilitate working into wet paint better than others. The fibres in highly absorbent papers soak up the washes and make any manipulation impossible, even immediately after they have been applied. Even better are papers that have been sized to such a degree that washes sit on the surface and dry slowly, rather than soak in.

Some techniques work better when the paint is very wet, while others are more effective when the paint has dried a little. Adding gum arabic to your washes can facilitate certain techniques, as it thickens the paint, increasing its viscosity so that it is less fluid. Thickening the paint prevents it from flowing freely and allows you to work into it more readily.

You can work into wet paint to depict any type of textured surface. You can remove paint by using textured fabrics, absorbent paper, man-made and natural sponges, to name but a few.

You can also make marks in wet paint by using a variety of tools that you might not normally associate with painting, such as combs, palette knives, pieces of stiff card, or the wooden end of your brushes. These are all excellent for this purpose, as is the relatively new range of rubber paint-shaping tools. Pressing fabrics, paper, and even aluminium kitchen foil or clear film (plastic wrap) all create interesting textures that you could not achieve using an ordinary brush.

When a wash is partially dry, dropping water or paint into it results in an effect known as a back-run (sometimes called the cauliflower effect). This can be put to good use when painting cloudy skies or flowers, as it creates a crinkled, often highly pigmented edge as the wetter paint pushes into the drier paint. A similar effect can be seen when paint that has collected in a puddle on buckled paper dries at a much slower rate than paint on the surrounding area.

Lifting off colour

There will be many occasions during your painting when you find that you need to remove some colour from your work – either to make minor corrections or simply to soften tones and edges. The methods shown below are particularly useful for lifting out clouds from a blue sky – but remember to turn the paper or sponge around in your hand each time you use it in order to find a clean area, otherwise you run the risk of dabbing paint back on.

Absorbent paper
First, lay a wash. While it is still wet, blot off any excess paint with a scrunched-up piece of clean, absorbent tissue or a paper towel.

Sponge
You can also lift off colour from a wet wash using a sponge. This gives more texture, as the texture of the sponge is impressed into the wet wash.

Pressing materials into wet paint

You can create interesting textures by pressing things into wet paint and removing them once the paint is dry. The results are a little unpredictable, but well worth experimenting with. Two possible materials are shown below, but you can easily come up with others from readily available household items. Lace, soft absorbent fabrics, such as cotton and felt, thick wool: experiment to see how many different effects you can create with whatever you have to hand.

Clear film

1 Scrunch up a piece of clear film (plastic wrap) in your fingers and gently press it into a wet watercolour wash. Leave it to dry.

2 When the paint is dry, carefully remove the clear film. The lines of the scrunched-up food wrap are clearly visible in the dry paint.

Aluminium kitchen foil

1 Scrunch up a piece of cooking foil and press it into a wet wash. Leave to dry.

2 When the paint is dry, carefully remove the foil. This creates crisper, sharper lines than the food wrap.

Practice exercise: **Graffiti-style abstract**

Remember how much fun you had as a child, messing around with poster paints and coming home with your fingers stained with bright, primary colours? This exercise is all about recapturing that sense of fun and excitement and getting a feel for how wet watercolour paint behaves. The result is an abstract mass of colour and texture, rather like graffiti sprayed on to a wall.

Feel free to experiment with materials other than the ones shown here: there are no limits to what you can use. Work quickly while the paint is still wet. Above all, don't try to plan ahead, simply react to the way the paint flows and puddles on the paper.

Materials
- *300lb (640gsm) rough watercolour paper*
- *Watercolour paints: alizarin crimson, cobalt blue, burnt sienna, ultramarine blue, cadmium yellow*
- *Watercolour pigments: alizarin crimson*
- *Brushes: old brush for masking, medium round*
- *Masking fluid and tape*
- *Kitchen paper*
- *Toothbrush*
- *Card*
- *Cotton bud*

1 Brush on random swirls of masking fluid and leave to dry. Cut abstract shapes from masking tape and press them on to the paper. Wash alizarin crimson and cobalt blue on to the paper, allowing the colours to merge.

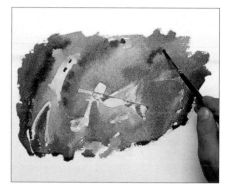

2 While the first washes are still wet, brush on burnt sienna and ultramarine blue, again allowing the colours to run together and merge on the paper in a completely random way. Tilt the board to facilitate this.

3 Brush on more alizarin crimson and dab a piece of kitchen paper onto the paper to lift off and soften colour.

4 You have now established a mass of abstract wet colours into which you can work.

▶

5 Using thick paint straight from the tube, brush on a few long strokes of cadmium yellow. This gives an impasto-like texture similar to oil paint.

6 Drag an old toothbrush over the yellow lines to spread and diffuse them. Because the bristles of the toothbrush are stiff and the paint is relatively thick, you can clearly see the marks that are left behind – an unusual way of adding texture to a watercolour.

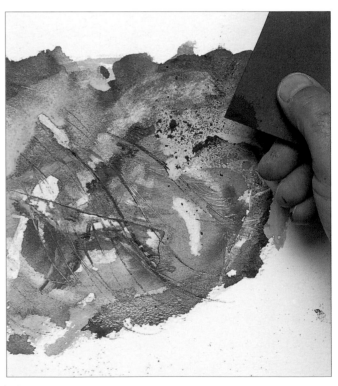

7 Take a small piece of card and scrape into the wet paint, dragging it from one colour into the next. The card is flexible, so you can make curved lines, while its thin edge allows you to create lines that are clearly defined. An old, cut-up credit card would have the same effect.

8 Pick up a little powder pigment on a piece of card and, gently tapping it with your finger, lightly sprinkle the pigment on to the paper. Note how the pigment colour spreads and blurs in damp areas but remains on the surface, creating an impasto-like texture, in dry parts.

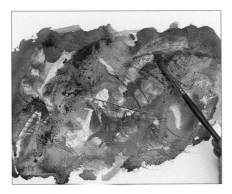

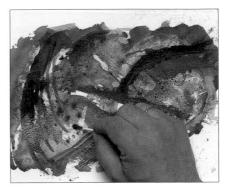

9 Dip a brush in clean water and brush over the pigment particles to blur and spread them. The more water you have on the brush, the further the powder will spread and the paler the colour will become.

10 Pull off the masking tape and rub off the fluid to reveal small areas of bright white. Brush more alizarin crimson on to selected areas of the paper and, while it is still wet, drag a toothbrush through it as before.

11 Dip a cotton bud in ultramarine blue paint and dot it on to the paper to make more clearly defined marks in selected areas.

The finished painting

This is a completely abstract, explosive riot of colour and texture. It was not pre-planned in any way, but was created by the artist responding to the way the wet paint behaved on the paper. Exercises like this will teach you a lot about manipulating paint and free you from any hang-ups about having to paint lifelike subjects.

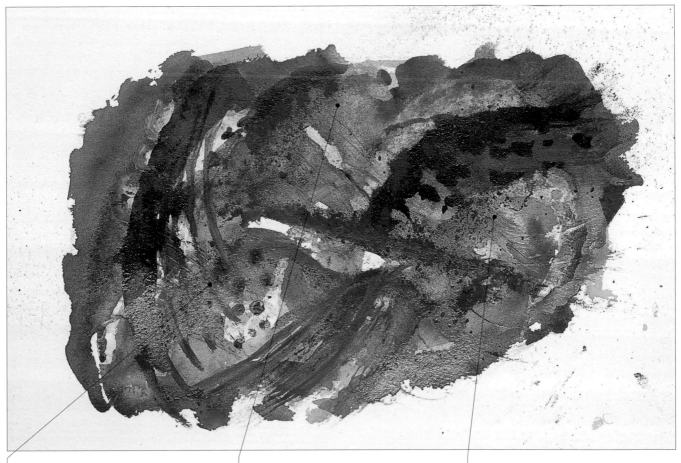

Clear lines and dots are created by scraping into the paint with card and dotting on colour with a cotton bud.

Allowing the paint to merge wet into wet creates soft background colour.

Using thick cadmium yellow paint straight from the tube creates an impasto-like effect.

Sgraffito

The technical name for scratching into dry paint comes from the Italian, *graffiare*, which means to scratch. Sgraffito can be used to reveal white paper beneath a wash, and is a good way to create highlights, such as sunlight on water. It can also be used to scratch through one layer of colour to reveal the layer beneath.

Paint can be scratched into using a variety of sharp implements. A scalpel or craft (utility) knife is useful for scratching fine lines, as are sharpened brush handles, paper clips and even your fingernails. For larger areas, abrasive paper is very effective; experiment with fine and harsh grades of sandpaper for different results.

You can also use sgraffito to remove small areas of paint to correct minor mistakes – for example, if you want to neaten an edge or the outline of an object. To do this, scrape gently, using the edge of the knife blade rather than the point, so that the paper is not torn and the scraped area remains flat.

All these techniques work better if the paint sits on the paper surface, rather than soaking into it to any depth, so try to avoid using sgraffito with staining colours such as alizarin crimson, viridian or phthalocyanine blue. Needless to say, it is best to use sgraffito on heavy paper (say, 300lb/640gsm) as it is less likely to tear, and on top of dry washes.

Scalpel or craft knife
To scratch fine lines, such as highlights on water, use the tip of a scalpel or craft (utility) knife, pulling the blade sideways to avoid slicing into the paper and damaging it.

Fine-grade abrasive paper
Stroke the paper over the surface of the dry paint. This is particularly effective on rough watercolour paper, as the paint remains in the troughs but is removed from the higher ridges.

Coarse-grade abrasive paper
Because the sand particles on coarse paper are bigger, the sgraffito lines are further apart. You can also fold the paper to create a crisp edge, enabling you to scratch off sharp lines.

Practice exercise: **Conch shell**

This conch shell contains a number of different textures, from hard, raised ridges and points to the mottled surface of some of the flatter areas and the porcelain smoothness of the inside. The following exercise gives you the chance to practise two methods of sgraffito, using abrasive paper for general areas of texture and a scalpel or craft (utility) knife for the crisp, sharp ridges on the outer side of the shell.

Materials
- *2B pencil*
- *300lb (640gsm) NOT watercolour paper*
- *Watercolour paints: yellow ochre, Payne's grey, alizarin crimson, raw umber*
- *Brushes: medium round*
- *Medium-grade abrasive paper*
- *Scalpel or craft (utility) knife*

The set-up
Arrange the shell at an interesting angle, so that you can see both the hard, spiky outer shell and the smooth, slightly shiny interior. This provides an attractive contrast of textures and makes it easier to appreciate the form of the object.

1 Using a 2B pencil, lightly sketch the shell to establish the general outline shape and the main ridges. Using a medium round brush, establish the overall colour with pale washes of yellow ochre, Payne's grey and a little alizarin crimson, allowing the colours to blend together on the paper and create a surface with subtle variations in colour. Leave to dry.

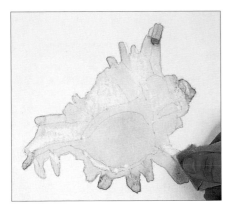

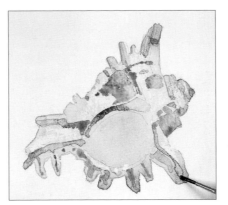

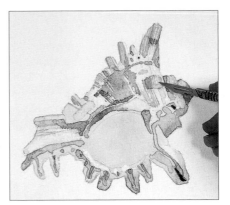

2 Take a small piece of medium-grade abrasive paper and stroke it over the paper to recreate the rough, pitted surface of the shell. (Leave the areas of smooth shell that lie deep within the interior untouched.) To scratch into small or tight areas of the image, fold the abrasive paper to make a crisp, sharp edge.

3 Mix a cool brown from yellow ochre and Payne's grey and paint the areas in shadow and some of the linear detail. When the paint dries, it will leave a rough texture on areas of the paper that have been rubbed with abrasive paper. Mix a dull pink from alizarin crimson and yellow ochre and paint the warm colours on the shell "lip". Leave to dry.

4 Using a sharp scalpel or craft (utility) knife, gently scratch into the dark paint until clean paper fibres are revealed, creating the ridges on the outer side of the shell.

The finished painting
The dense, cast shadow is painted in a darker, more pigmented mixture, which anchors the shell to the surface on which it rests, and also has the effect of throwing it into sharp relief. When painted over, the rough texture made by the abrasive paper creates a broken effect that contrasts well with the fine, crisp lines made with the point of the scalpel or craft-knife blade.

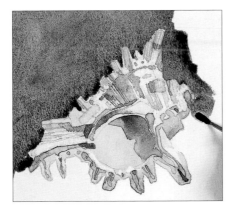

5 Mix a mid-toned grey from Payne's grey and a little yellow ochre and paint the shadow inside the shell. Mix a darker grey from Payne's grey and raw umber and wash in the background, painting very carefully around the shell.

A scalpel or craft (utility) knife is used to scratch off these crisp lines on the outside of the conch shell.

General areas of rough texture are created using medium-grade abrasive paper.

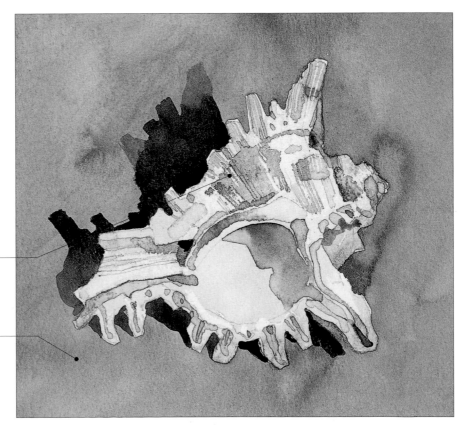

Body colour

Traditional transparent watercolour uses no white paint. Instead, you have to leave any areas of the painting that you want to be white, such as clouds or highlights sparkling on water, free of paint. Colours are made paler by adding more water.

The white of the paper also serves to reflect light back through transparent coloured washes. Depending on the depth of the colour, this can make them appear lighter or darker. Because the washes are transparent, when one colour is painted on top of another the underlying colour will always show through. This makes it impossible in pure watercolour to paint a light colour on top of a dark one.

Body colour is somewhat different. White and pale shades are obtained by adding white pigment, which adds "body" to the paint and renders it opaque. Chinese white, which is made from zinc oxide and gum arabic, was traditionally used as body colour. It is a dense white with a very high tinting strength. A good alternative, which many artists use, is white gouache.

You can use body colour straight from the tube to create highlights and details that would normally have been made by preserving the white of the paper – catchlights in people's eyes, for example, or white whiskers on a cat. You can also mix it with transparent watercolour paint to produce light, opaque pastel tints that can then be painted on top of dark colours. This is particularly useful when you want to add subtle pale details or textures – for example, by spattering white paint on to the support to represent falling snow in a snow scene.

Body colour comes into its own when you are working on a coloured or tinted ground because it enables you to use light tones and colours without them being influenced by the underlying ground colour, which can completely overpower pale, transparent washes.

Body colour can also be used to correct mistakes – perhaps highlights that you have forgotten to leave white, or even entire passages that you want to cover up and repaint. Use it cautiously, however, as too much can look heavy and deaden the lovely translucent quality for which pure watercolour is renowned.

You need a degree of competence and flair to mix the two techniques of body colour and transparent washes. It is easy for the two techniques to jar and work at odds with one another, but if used carefully, body colour can extend the creative possibilites of watercolour as a medium, and will bring another dimension to your watercolours.

Light watercolour over dark watercolour
When a paler or lighter transparent watercolour paint is applied over the top of a darker paint, the underlying dark wash will show through.

Light gouache over dark watercolour
When a paler or lighter watercolour paint is combined with Chinese white gouache, the mixture becomes opaque. It then becomes possible to apply a lighter colour on top of a darker one.

Practice exercise: **Painting light on dark**

A lighter blue pattern on a rich, dark blue background: in pure watercolour, the only ways to paint the pattern on this little embossed vase would be either to mask the light areas, which might look too bright when the masking is removed, or to paint the light areas first, and then carefully paint the darker blue around them, which is quite a fiddly process.

With body colour, however, things are much simpler. By mixing Chinese white gouache with transparent watercolour paints, you can create pale, opaque mixtures that can be painted on top of the dark, underlying colours. The opaque pattern also contrasts well with the translucent watercolour used to paint the blue of the vase.

The set-up
Tiny orange flowers were chosen to contrast with the rich blue of the vase – orange and blue are complementary

colours and they work well together. Positioning a table lamp to one side of the vase helps to pick up the texture of the embossed pattern.

Materials
- *B pencil*
- *140lb (300gsm) rough watercolour paper, unstretched*
- *Watercolour paints: ultramarine blue, burnt sienna, cadmium lemon, cadmium red, cadmium yellow*
- *Gouache paints: Chinese white*
- *Brushes: medium round, large wash*

1 Using a B pencil, sketch the subject. Don't attempt to draw every single leaf and flower: a light indication of the general areas is sufficient.

2 Mix a rich blue from ultramarine blue with a little burnt sienna. Using a medium round brush, paint the vase, adding a little more burnt sienna for the right-hand side of the vase, which is in shade. Dilute the mixture for the shadow cast by the vase.

3 Mix a dull green from cadmium lemon, ultramarine blue and a little cadmium red and brush in the broad shapes of the leaves. Add more cadmium lemon to the mixture and paint the lighter leaves. Dot the same mixture over the unopened buds.

4 Add a little cadmium yellow to the dilute shadow mixture used in Step 2 and, using a medium round brush, brush it over the background to relieve the whiteness. Mix an orangey green from cadmium lemon, ultramarine blue and cadmium red and start to put in the flower buds that are just starting to open. Mix a pale, opaque blue from ultramarine blue and Chinese white gouache and paint the pattern on the vase.

5 Add a tiny amount of burnt sienna to the opaque blue mixture and continue painting the pattern on the right-hand side of the vase. These subtle changes in tone help to establish which areas are in shade, as a result of which the vase begins to take on a more three-dimensional quality. Burnt sienna is also slightly orange in tone: shadow colours often contain a hint of a complementary colour.

▶

6 Mix a bright orange from cadmium red and cadmium yellow, and paint the tiny open flowers. Note how this use of complementary colours (the orange flowers against the blue of the vase) immediately makes the painting look more lively and dynamic.

7 Mix a dark green from ultramarine blue, burnt sienna and cadmium yellow and paint the darkest leaves. Mix a light green from cadmium yellow and ultramarine blue and paint the unopened buds. Mix orange from cadmium lemon, cadmium red and Chinese white gouache and paint the opening buds.

8 Add Chinese white gouache to the bright orange used in Step 6 to make it opaque. Use the mixture to paint the flowers that overhang the deep green leaves.

9 Mix a pale orange from cadmium yellow and cadmium red and brush it over the surface on which the vase sits. This will tone down the brightness and will provide a visual link to the colour of the flowers. Mix an opaque light green from cadmium lemon, ultramarine blue and Chinese white gouache and paint some light leaves over the dark ones.

The finished painting

Combining pure watercolour paint with Chinese white gouache makes it possible to paint light colours on top of dark ones. Because of its opacity, the body colour is also very effective in suggesting the embossed texture of the vase. Note also the effective use of the complementary colours blue and orange for the flowers.

Chinese white gouache has been used to tone down the bright orange of the flowers.

Pure watercolour paint is used for most of the vase. The translucency of the paint conveys the shiny glaze very effectively.

The opaque, pale blue mixture completely covers the underlying dark blue wash.

Scale and perspective

The further away something is from you, the smaller and less distinct it seems with the naked eye. In order to convincingly depict depth and recession, and so add a sense of realism to your work, you need to depict this shift in scale accurately. This is done by using a technique known as perspective.

At first sight, perspective may seem complex and confusing, but the basics are easy to understand and even a rudimentary grasp of the fundamentals will enable you to position elements in your work so that they appear to occupy their correct "space" in the composition.

As with any endeavour, planning is the key to success. You need to consider any perspective issues from the moment you begin a work and incorporate them from the outset. If you are unsure, make a sketch or a working drawing before you begin work on the painting. This will allow you to work out any problems in advance.

Aerial perspective

Sometimes known as atmospheric perspective, aerial perspective refers to the way the atmosphere combined with distance influences and affects what you see. Being able to identify and utilize these effects will enable you to paint realistic and convincing three-dimensional landscapes.

Four things are directly influenced by distance: these are texture, colour, tone and size. The most obvious of these is size. Objects gradually become smaller the further away from you they are. You can see this most clearly by looking along a row of identically sized telegraph poles, fence posts or trees.

Second, detail and textures become less evident with distance. Close-up texture and detail are often large and in sharp focus, while texture and detail that is further away is vague and less clearly defined.

Third, colours seen in the foreground and near distance appear bright and vibrant because the warm colours – reds, oranges and yellows – are in evidence. Colours in the far distance appear much less bright. They are also cooler and contain more blue and violet.

Finally, tonal contrast is dramatically reduced with distance, and sometimes it disappears completely, so that distant hills, for example, might appear as one pale mass.

These effects on size, detail and colour are caused by our own visual limitations. They are also caused by the gases, dust and moisture present in our atmosphere, which create a veil through which light has to filter. In addition, all these effects are directly influenced not only by the time of day, but also by the season of the year, the location, and the inherent local weather conditions.

The principles of aerial perspective apply not only to terra firma but also to the sky. Clouds appear larger when they are viewed immediately overhead. The sky alters colour too, being a warmer, deeper blue immediately overhead, gradually becoming paler and often with a cool yellow tinge as it falls towards the horizon and the far distance.

The effects of aerial perspective ▼
This simple landscape clearly illustrates the effects of aerial perspective and shows how atmosphere combined with distance influence the way we see things.

Colours in the foreground look warmer and brighter.

Clouds appear smaller the closer they are to the horizon.

Colours in the distance are cooler and less intense.

Detail is less apparent in the distance.

Tonal contrast is reduced in the background.

Detail is more apparent in the foreground.

A full range of tones can be seen in the foreground.

Linear perspective

Linear perspective is a system or device that allows you to create the illusion of three-dimensional space on a two-dimensional flat surface. The system is based on the principle that all parallel lines, known as perspective lines, when extended from any receding surface meet at a point in space known as the vanishing point.

The vanishing point is on what is known as the horizon line, which runs horizontally across the field of vision. The horizon line is also known as the eye level, because it always runs horizontally across the field of view at eye level, regardless of whether you are sitting or standing. All perspective lines that originate above the eye level run down to meet the vanishing point and all perspective lines that originate below the eye level run up to meet it. All vertical lines remain vertical.

The simplest form of perspective is single, or one-point, perspective. This occurs when all the receding perspective lines meet at one single point. The vanishing point in single-point perspective always coincides with your centre of vision, which is directly in front of you.

You can see the effect of single-point perspective by looking along a train track that runs straight away from you into the distance. The two rails are, in reality, consistently spaced the same distance apart, but because they are resting on the ground plane, which is receding away from you, the rails appear to converge the further away they get, eventually meeting when they reach the vanishing point.

A similar effect can be seen when you are standing in a straight road and looking into the distance along a row of identical houses. Using straight perspective lines to extend the roof line, the gutters, the top and bottom of the windows and doors, you will see that they all meet at the same vanishing point.

Parallel lines receding away from the viewer ▼
In this simple illustration of one-point perspective the trees – which, in reality, are all of similar size – appear to get smaller the further away they are. All perspective lines above eye level run down to the vanishing point (VP) and all perspective lines below eye level run up to the vanishing point.

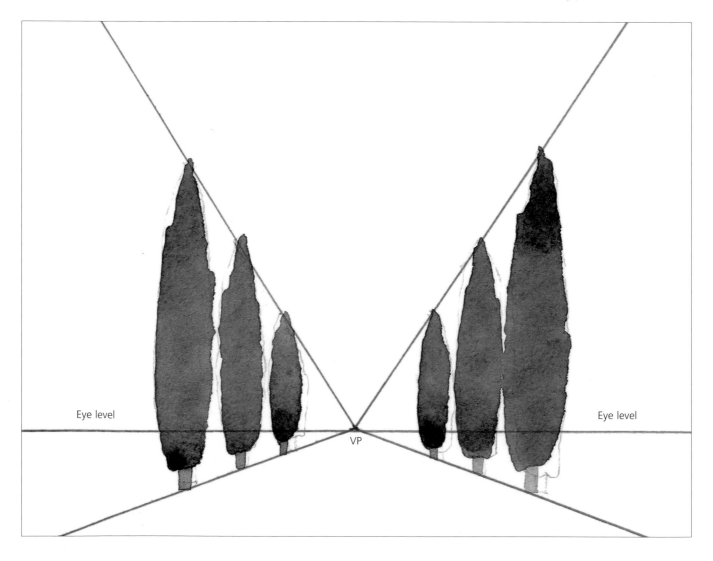

Eye level   VP   Eye level

Parallel lines receding to one side ▼

Here, all the elements on the front of the house are on the same plane and so they all meet at the same vanishing point.

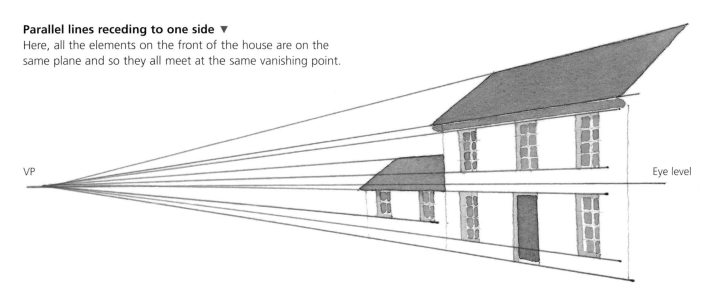

VP
Eye level

Subject below eye level ▼

As in the other examples shown on these two pages, a single vanishing point is all that is required in this view of a chess board, because the chess board is orientated with one side square to the viewer.

All the receding parallel lines on the board extend to the vanishing point. Because the board is below eye level, the perspective lines run up to meet the vanishing point. The width of each row of squares is arrived at by measurement; the depth of the board is also measured. Drawing a diagonal line from corner to corner of the board will help you to work out the depth of each row of squares, as the corners of these squares have to fall on the diagonal line.

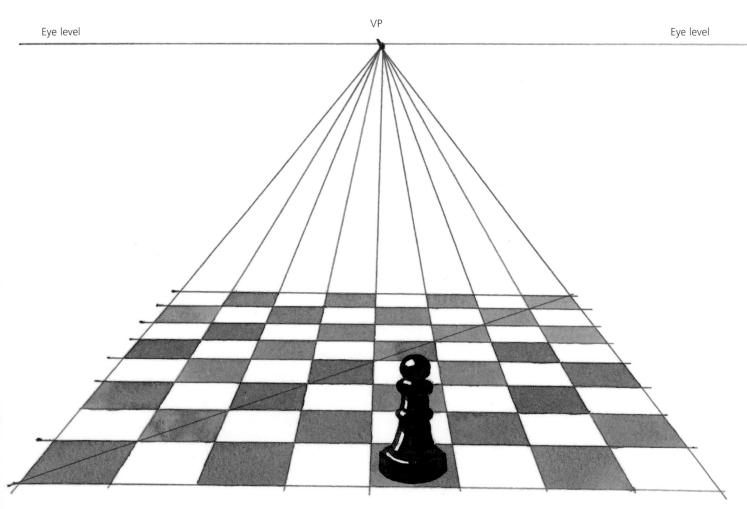

Eye level
VP
Eye level

Two-point perspective

If any two sides of an object can be seen at the same time, then two-point perspective comes into play. The principle remains the same as that discussed in one-point perspective, but because two surfaces are visible and both surfaces are at different angles, any parallel lines on those surfaces will eventually meet at their own vanishing point.

In two-point perspective, neither vanishing point falls at your centre of vision. Perspective lines on the right-hand side will converge at a vanishing point off to the right and perspective lines on the left-hand side will converge at a vanishing point off to the left. Even if you move to a position that is higher than your subject, the horizon line on which any vanishing points are situated will still run across your field of vision at eye level, so all perspective lines will run at an upwards angle to meet it. Similarly, if you move to a position below your subject, so that you are looking up at it, all perspective lines will run at a downwards angle to meet the horizon line.

Two planes visible – two-point perspective ▼
Two-point perspective needs to be taken into consideration when you can see two or three sides (planes) of a rectangular object at the same time. Here, we see two sides of a row of coloured boxes, all of which are orientated the same way. The perspective lines of each side of each box extend to the same vanishing point.

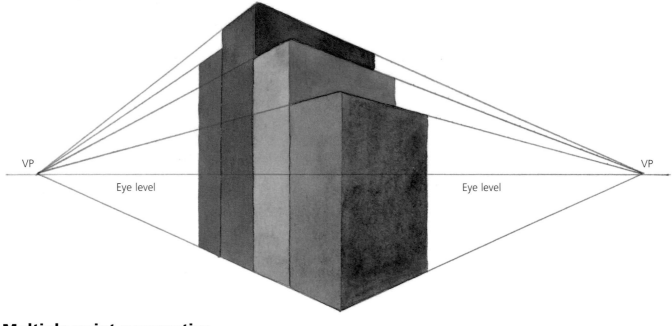

Multiple-point perspective

When several objects are arranged at different heights and angles, then multiple-point perspective comes into play. It looks a little more complicated, but the rules remain the same. Each object needs to be treated as a separate entity and its vanishing points and perspective lines should be plotted accordingly.

Objects at different angles – multiple-point perspective ▶
Here, three box-like shapes are resting on what might be a table top. Each box is facing in a slightly different direction, so each one needs to have separate vanishing points – as does the table top, which is orientated differently to the boxes.

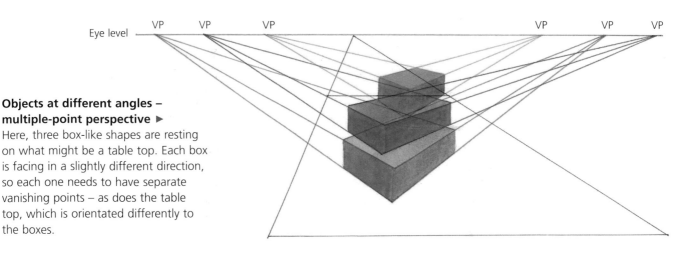

Drawing curved and circular objects in perspective

Understanding the principles of perspective enables you to represent not only simple box-like structures, as in the examples that we've looked at so far, but also highly complex-shaped objects that possess curved, as well as flat, surfaces.

Curved and circular objects become ellipses when they are seen in perspective. To draw them accurately, first work out the area they occupy using squares and rectangles, which are also in perspective.

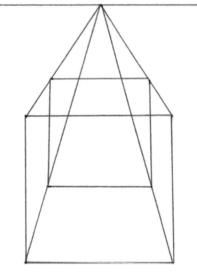

1 First work out the area that the object (in this case, a cylinder) occupies, using simple squares or rectangles seen in perspective. Here the cylinder is viewed from directly in front and slightly above. A simple cube seen in single-point perspective indicates the position and approximate size of the cylinder.

2 Find the centre of the top of the cube by drawing lines from corner to corner. Further divide the top of the cube into quarters by drawing a line (A–B) parallel to the front of the cube through the centre point and by drawing another line (C) through the centre point to line up with the vanishing point (VP). Do the same to the base of the cube.

3 From point C on the front edge of the top of the cube, measure halfway to the corner (D). Drop a line at right angles to E, the same length as the measurement C–D. Position a compass point at C, with the radius set to E. Swing the compass from here to find points F. Draw a line from F to line up with the vanishing point (VP). Repeat on the base.

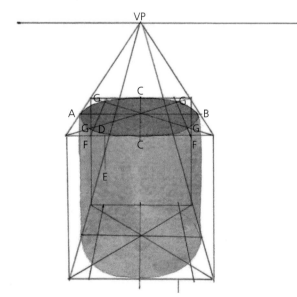

4 The exact curvature of the top of the cylinder is established by drawing a curved line to connect points A, B and C at point G – through the points where the line F–VP intersects the lines that run from corner to corner. Follow the same procedure to find the curvature at the bottom of the cylinder.

Composition

The way in which all the visual elements within a painting are put together is known as composition. The factors that govern composition include shape, scale, perspective, colour and texture. The purpose of composition is to manipulate and lead the eye while finding a pleasing visual balance of all these elements. Balance does not mean visual symmetry: shape can be offset with texture or colour with scale.

Composition can also be used to create mood. A composition can evoke feelings of heaviness and oppression, or be airy, light and uplifting. There are certain rules to composition, but breaking these rules often gives a work a certain edge that can lift it from the mundane and pedestrian into something much more eyecatching.

Formats

The first thing you need to consider is what shape (or format) to make your painting. The three main formats are vertical (also know as portrait), horizontal (also known as landscape) and square. Needless to say, portraits can be painted on landscape-format supports and landscapes on portrait ones. Two other formats that are often used are round (or oval) and a wider horizontal format known as panoramic.

Catching the light ▼
The roughly square format suits the subject perfectly: the neck and head curve around, balancing the bulk detail of the body.

Paul Dyson ©

Robin ▼

A wide, panoramic format has been chosen for this painting of a robin on a branch. At first glance, it might seem that the subject is quite insignificant and does not warrant such an extreme format, but exaggerating the width of the painting has introduced a tension that would be lacking if the more usual landscape format had been used. The clever device of the arching branch, which runs the entire width of the image, prevents the picture from appearing one-sided: the eye wanders along it and across the picture, but always returns to the brilliant flash of red on the bird's breast.

Seaside steps ▶

The vertical format of this work again suits the subject. The eye is pulled along the length of the craft and up the steps towards the building. The golden yellow stonework pulls the eye down to the bottom of the picture and the circular journey begins again.

Etretat, Normandy ▼

The image of these cliffs in northern France sits comfortably in the horizontal format. The curve of the waterline sweeps the eye around to the cliffs and into the painting. At the base of the cliffs, the viewer's attention is caught by the dark ripples and reflection in the water; these in turn bring the eye down to the breaking waves and round again.

Dividing the picture area

The principle of good composition is that nothing should dominate to such an extent that it holds the viewer's attention completely and exclusively – although, of course, there are occasions when artists deliberately choose to do precisely that. Dividing the picture area up and deciding exactly what should go where can be difficult, but there are some general guidelines that will help you.

Over the centuries, artists have devised ways of positioning the main pictorial elements and focal points on an invisible grid around specific positions within the picture area. The classic compositional device, and the one that is considered to be the ideal division of an area and aesthetically superior to others, is based on the golden section – the term used for a mathematical formula devised by Euclid and developed by Plato. Also known as divine proportion, it states that a line or area can be divided so that the "smaller part is to the larger as the larger part is to the whole".

A simpler and less rigid grid, which is easier to follow and use, is made by splitting the picture area into thirds, regardless of the format chosen. This is done by simply dividing the image area into three, both horizontally and vertically, which gives a grid consisting of nine sections, with lines crossing at four points. The theory is that positioning major elements of the image near these lines or at their intersections will result in a pleasing image. As with the golden section, the formula is a good starting point on which to base your compositions.

It is generally considered inadvisable to position your subject in the very centre of the picture area, as it makes for a rather static image. However, a feeling of calmness and inactivity are sometimes exactly what the subject requires. Be guided by your instincts, even if they sometimes appear to be going against the rules.

Beach, early morning ▼
This simple painting of a beach umbrella and sun loungers silhouetted in the early morning sun is firmly based on the rule of thirds. The umbrella provides a strong vertical element approximately a third of the way in from the right-hand side, while the shoreline and sun loungers provide a horizontal element approximately one third of the way up from the bottom of the picture. These dark shapes are balanced by the empty area of water.

The Tuileries, Paris ▲
The chairs and litter bin are the centre of interest and are loosely positioned on the intersecting grid lines to the right of the image while the top third of the painting is filled with row upon row of leafless trees. Together, they balance the empty space in the bottom left of the image.

Flamenco guitarist ▶
Although it is perhaps not immediately apparent, this portrait is also based around the rule of thirds. The head of the guitarist, the bulk of the guitar body, and the tuning head are all positioned at points where the grid lines intersect, while the figure's torso and the ornate pillar are placed a third of the way in from the left- and right-hand sides respectively.

Leading the eye

In a successful composition, the viewer's eye should be directed towards the image's centre of interest and encouraged to linger on the picture. Introducing curves and lines within the picture, either real or implied, are one way of doing this. Obvious examples of this might be a road leading up to a building, a river snaking its way through a landscape, or a line of trees receding into the distance.

All compositions are either "open" or "closed". A closed composition is one in which the eye is held within the picture area. It may be induced to move around from object to object, but essentially its focus is firmly held. An example of a closed composition might be a view from a dark interior through a window, with the window surround acting as a frame within a frame. An open gateway or tree trunks and branches might serve the same purpose. An open composition encourages the eye to move around the image, but also seems to suggest that the image continues well beyond the boundaries of the picture area. Many landscapes are perfect examples of open compositions.

Another strong compositional device, especially when painting landscapes, is the positioning of the horizon. This can have a profound effect on the mood of the image. Landscapes can be given extra impact by making the horizon very high within the picture area or even eliminating it altogether. Clouds can also be an important compositional consideration, providing large, eye-catching shapes in what might otherwise be an empty space.

Louvre Museum, Paris ▲
This is a good example of a closed composition. The eye is unavoidably pulled into the work past the sculpture and out the window into the centre of the image. The dark window surround acts as a visual barrier and encourages the eye to linger in the central area.

◄ Clos de Vosges
These weathered gate pillars act as a frame within a frame, drawing the eye through to the vineyard and buildings beyond. Because the pillars are placed centrally, the eye can move around within the rest of the painting. If they were placed closer to the edge of the image, the composition would seem more closed and confined.

Springs ▼

Rules are made to be broken. Placing the horizon line across the centre of an image is generally considered bad practice, but it can be made to work. Here, the strong sense of perspective leads the eye into the centre of the image.

The visual activity on the horizon line acts as a buffer, pushing the eyes out to either side. The bottom part of the image is roughly divided into thirds. The wide expanse of sky is broken by the row of telegraph poles.

Mont St Michel ▶

This is an example of both an open composition and breaking the so-called rules about where to position the horizon. The landscape and building are placed low in the picture area, with the horizon running across the image about a quarter of the way up. This has the effect of drawing attention to the sky, which is a featureless pale blue. One would not normally expect so much emphasis to be given to seemingly empty space, but in this instance the sheer size and weight of the sky provide a counterbalance to the visual activity in the lower part of the painting. The result is a powerful, atmospheric image that is possessed of a perfect spirit of place.

Index